THE IVP NEW TESTAMENT COMMENTARY SERIES

1-3 John

Marianne Meye Thompson

Grant R. Osborne
series editor

D. Stuart Briscoe
Haddon Robinson
consulting editors

INTERVARSITY PRESS
DOWNERS GROVE, ILLINOIS, USA
LEICESTER, ENGLAND

InterVarsity Press
P.O. Box 1400, Downers Grove, Illinois 60515, U.S.A.
38 De Montfort Street, Leicester LE1 7GP, England

© *1992 by Marianne Meye Thompson*

InterVarsity Press, U.S.A., is the book-publishing division of InterVarsity Christian Fellowship, a student movement active on campus at hundreds of universities, colleges and schools of nursing in the United States of America, and a member movement of the International Fellowship of Evangelical Students. For information about local and regional activities, write Public Relations Dept., InterVarsity Christian Fellowship, 6400 Schroeder Rd., P.O. Box 7895, Madison, WI 53707-7895.

Inter-Varsity Press, England, is the book-publishing division of the Universities and Colleges Christian Fellowship (formerly the Inter-Varsity Fellowship), a student movement linking Christian Unions in universities and colleges throughout the United Kingdom and the Republic of Ireland, and a member movement of the International Fellowship of Evangelical Students. For information about local and national activities write to UCCF, 38 De Montfort Street, Leicester LE1 7GP.

USA ISBN 0-8308-1819-7
UK ISBN 0-85111-671-X

Printed in the United States of America ∞

Library of Congress Cataloging-in-Publication Data

Thompson, Marianne Meye.
  1-3 John/Marianne Meye Thompson.
    p.   cm.— (The IVP New Testament commentary series)
  Includes bibliographical references.
  ISBN 0-8308-1819-7
    1. Bible.   N.T. Epistles of John—Commentaries.   I. Title.
  II. Series.
  BS2805.3.T45   1992
  227'.9407—dc20   *91-45910*
                                                                CIP

British Library Cataloguing in Publication Data

A catalogue record for this book is available from the British Library.

17	16	15	14	13	12	11	10	9	8	7	6	5	4	3	2	1
06	05	04	03	02	01	00	99	98	97	96	95	94	93	92		

For Allison and Annelise

*"No greater joy can I have than this,
to hear that my children follow the truth."*
(3 John 4)

General Preface

In an age of proliferating commentary series, one might easily ask why add yet another to the seeming glut. The simplest answer is that no other series has yet achieved what we had in mind—a series to and from the church, that seeks to move from the text to its contemporary relevance and application.

No other series offers the unique combination of solid, biblical exposition and helpful explanatory notes in the same user-friendly format. No other series has tapped the unique blend of scholars and pastors who share both a passion for faithful exegesis and a deep concern for the church. Based on the New International Version of the Bible, one of the most widely used modern translations, the IVP New Testament Commentary Series builds on the NIV's reputation for clarity and accuracy. Individual commentators indicate clearly whenever they depart from the standard translation as required by their understanding of the original Greek text.

The series contributors represent a wide range of theological traditions, united by a common commitment to the authority of Scripture for

Christian faith and practice. Their efforts here are directed toward apply-ing the unchanging message of the New Testament to the ever-changing world in which we live.

Readers will find in each volume, not only traditional discussions of authorship and backgrounds, but useful summaries of principal themes and approaches to contemporary application. To bridge the gap between commentaries that stress the flow of an author's argument but skip over exegetical nettles and those that simply jump from one difficulty to another, we have developed our unique format that expounds the text in uninterrupted form on the upper portion of each page while dealing with other issues underneath in verse-keyed notes. To avoid clutter we have also adopted a social studies note system that keys references to the bibliography.

We offer the series in hope that pastors, students, Bible teachers and small group leaders of all sorts will find it a valuable aid—one that stretches the mind and moves the heart to ever-growing faithfulness and obedience to our Lord Jesus Christ.

Author's Preface

There are many to thank for their support, encouragement and assistance over the years that I worked on this commentary. I extend my thanks to Bethany Community Church of Seattle, to the women of Highland Park Presbyterian Church of Dallas and to various groups of La Crescenta Presbyterian Church for allowing me to try out some of my material in various forms. To my students who studied the epistles with me, and especially to those who read the commentary in draft and gave me helpful responses and feedback, I am grateful. I am indebted to the Board of Trustees of Fuller Theological Seminary for the granting of sabbatical leave that enabled the completion of this volume. Thanks are also due to the staff at InterVarsity Press and to the editors who read this book in draft. Their many suggestions have, I hope, improved the volume, and in any case no blame is to be assigned to them for any deficiencies that remain.

I should also like to thank my colleagues at Fuller Seminary who make our service together a joy and inspire me to faith, hope and love. As I think of these friends, there is both joy and sadness. It is a special pleasure to be able to name my husband, John, among my colleagues here, and to thank him for his encouragement and support in this and in all our life together. But it was during the final stages of finishing this work that we received the news of the untimely death of our colleague Bob Guelich. His warm friendship, collegial spirit and deep faith will be sorely missed by us all. I hope that in some way this commentary can help to further these same qualities in the church of Christ, for which Bob cared so passionately.

The writing of this commentary spanned a period of several years, marked on either end by the birth of our daughters, to whom this work is dedicated. No dedication could be more fitting. For they have helped bring to life every word in the epistles about the joy, love and confidence we have as God's children. It is our prayer that what they have taught us in their infancy, we may also teach them to know in maturity, that together we may be found to walk as companions of the One who is true.

Introduction

When a number of reformers, including Luther and Zwingli, met at the Colloquy of Marburg in 1529 to discuss theological differences, one of the main topics of discussion was the significance of the Lord's Supper. Luther voiced his disagreement with Zwingli and those of the Reformed confession in the statement "We have a different spirit" (see Luther 1971:70). Years later, when the Swiss theologian, Karl Barth, was teaching in Germany in the 1930s, all professors were required to open every lecture with the so-called Hitler salute and to sign a loyalty oath to Hitler and the government. Barth expressed his reservations to those Christian professors who signed the oath with the statement "We have different beliefs, different spirits and a different God" (Busch 1976:242).

We can go back in time nearly two millennia, to a community known to us from the pages of the three short epistles of the New Testament commonly called 1, 2 and 3 John. It was a community torn by conflict and marred by schism. The two sides of the dispute were represented by those loyal to the "Elder," the author of these epistles, and those who had left the community (1 Jn 2:19). The Elder could well have said of those who departed, "We have different beliefs, different spirits and a different God" (compare 1 Jn 4:1-6).

Looking back over history, we would probably say that Luther overstated the case when he argued that the Lutheran and Reformed confessions "had a different spirit." But the events of history proved Barth's statement to be prophetic: the German Christians, loyal to the Third Reich, surely had a different spirit than those who resisted Hitler's policies. And what about the Elder and his opponents? Have his judgments that those who left his congregation manifested the spirit of antichrist been sustained by history? What was at stake that elicited such a blanket condemnation of his opponents? Did they differ, like Luther and Zwingli, on an important but not essential tenet of the faith? Or were the disagreements between the Elder and the secessionists so great and so central to the faith that no compromise was possible?

In order to answer this question, we must seek to reconstruct the situation and issues behind the epistles. By doing this we can discern what was at stake for the Elder in these disputes, and so sharpen our minds and hearts to be aware of similar issues facing our churches today. The better we can ascertain what problems faced these early Christians, the better we can understand how to cope with similar problems still facing the church today.

I. The Occasion and Purpose of the Epistles
Each of the epistles testifies to an underlying conflict. However, while the situations of the readers addressed in 1 and 2 John are closely related, and perhaps identical, it is not so clear that 3 John was written to help its readers face the same crisis. Accordingly, we shall discuss 1 and 2 John together, and then ask how 3 John fits into the picture.

A. The Occasion and Purpose of 1 and 2 John
The Situation of the Readers To understand the Johannine community we should envision a network of smaller congregations or house churches, sharing a theological heritage and historical roots. Within one (or perhaps several) of these smaller churches there are theological conflicts (1 Jn 4:1-6; 5:5-8; 2 Jn 7-10) and social rifts (1 Jn 2:18-26; 4:1; 2 Jn 7). The Elder (2 Jn 1; 3 Jn 1), who has pastoral responsibility for

the larger community and is probably a member of the smaller congregation in which the division has occurred, is now writing both to interpret the split that has torn his church and to warn other congregations about the problem.

The Nature of the Problem But what exactly is the problem? Broadly speaking, we may describe the conflict as focused on the *nature and implications of salvation.* Those who left the community—the "secessionists"—apparently held the view that those who were the "children of God" (1 Jn 3:1-2) attained a spiritual status by being "born of God" (3:9-10) that not only delivered them from the guilt and power of sin but actually rendered them sinless. They claimed to be without sin and to have attained a state of perfect righteousness (1 Jn 1:8, 10). In this regard they were like Jesus (2:1-2; 3:2) and like God, whose children they were (3:1-3).

A consequence of the secessionists' belief in their full and present righteousness was what amounts to a denial of the significance of the atonement of Christ. They agreed that once they had needed God's forgiveness through Christ. But having been purified of their sin and born of God, they had been granted a status in which they no longer needed atonement, for they were no longer guilty of or subject to sin. And where there is no sin, there is no need of confession or atonement. Moreover, since righteousness was a status already attained, there was no call to grow in righteousness or purity or knowledge of God. These were the present possession of the children of God. While the Elder agrees that the children of God have received the gift of God's salvation, he disagrees with the secessionists that they have attained this fully in the present life (3:1-3); that being "children of God" makes no demands on the way they live (2:6); and that they have ceased to need forgiveness (1:8—2:2).

Thus the letters of 1 and 2 John are as much about Christian spirituality and conduct as they are about doctrine and belief. However, they have long been viewed as dealing primarily with a doctrinal dispute about the person of Jesus (Christology), a dispute that ultimately led to the fracturing of the church. Efforts to find historical parallels to the teaching addressed in 1 and 2 John have focused on the problems of Christology. A brief review will show how the parallels might shed light on the situation that occasioned the Johannine epistles.

Historical Parallels to the Teaching of the Secessionists Three dominant theories about the nature of the heresy in 1 and 2 John have arisen:

1. The opponents are Cerinthians. One of the oldest understandings of the epistles is that they are directed against the teachings of Cerinthus (see Stott 1988:48-55). According to tradition, Cerinthus was the archenemy of the apostle John in Ephesus, but we know little about Cerinthus. As summarized by Irenaeus (in *Against All Heresies* 1.26.1), Cerinthus' Christology distinguished between Jesus and Christ. *Jesus* was merely a human being like all others, although noteworthy for his righteousness, prudence and wisdom. *Christ* (the Messiah) was a heavenly and spiritual being who descended upon the merely human Jesus at his baptism and departed at the crucifixion. Thus the human Jesus, not the heavenly, divine Christ, suffered and died.

If the secessionists' teaching is understood against this background, then the statement that Jesus came "not . . . by water only, but by water and blood" (1 Jn 5:6) might be taken as an affirmation of the union of "Jesus" and "Christ" throughout his entire life, from his baptism (water) to his death (blood). There was no temporary merger of two distinct beings, and it was indeed the Messiah who died on the cross. The affirmation that "Jesus Christ has come in the flesh" (1 Jn 4:2; 2 Jn 7) would then be understood to emphasize the permanent union of Jesus and the Christ.

But there are other ways of reading these verses. Moreover, the records that we have of Cerinthus' teaching lack certain features (such as claims to be without sin) that figure prominently in 1 John, while other ideas attributed to Cerinthus by Irenaeus are never mentioned or refuted in 1 John. And some of Cerinthus' views, such as his belief that Jesus exceeded all his contemporaries in righteousness, actually seem closer to those of the author of 1 John, who holds up Jesus' righteousness as an example to imitate (2:6; 3:7), than to the views of the dissidents themselves.

2. The opponents are Docetists. One tendency in early Christian thought was what has come to be known as "docetism" (from the Greek word *dokein* meaning "to seem"), which denied the reality of the Incarnation by claiming that Jesus only "seemed" to be human. Such teaching is documented quite early in the history of the church, for Ignatius of Antioch (early second century) wrote several epistles to churches in Asia Minor warning his readers against docetizing tendencies. Ignatius reminds his readers that Jesus did not merely seem to be human, or merely appear to suffer and to die. He really suffered, and he really died. Some scholars have read 1 John 4:2 ("Jesus Christ has come in the flesh") as an insistence that Jesus was indeed a human being of flesh and blood, and so have taken this verse as part of the epistle's attack on a docetic Christology.

But it is not obvious that in the statement "Jesus Christ has come in the flesh" (1 Jn 4:2) the accent falls on the word *flesh*. Even if it does, it is not clear that it counters the view that Jesus only *seemed* to have a body of flesh. It could, for example, be directed against a group which argued that there had never been an Incarnation at all or who, like Cerinthus, held that the Incarnation was merely temporary. While "Jesus Christ has come in the flesh" does affirm the reality of Jesus' humanity, it is much more difficult to deduce the views against which such a statement is directed.

3. The opponents are Gnostics. The early church was confronted by various forms of the teaching that we label "Gnosticism." Cerinthus' views were of Gnostic orientation, and some Gnostics were also Docetists. Among the features of Gnosticism that have parallels in the Johannine epistles are the dualism of light and darkness and of truth and falsehood; claims to special union with or special knowledge of God; the view that the Christian is begotten of God, and that certain human beings have a "spiritual seed" implanted within them (1 Jn 3:9); and claims to sinlessness (1 Jn 1:8, 10). Some Gnostic Christologies held that in Jesus two natures (spiritual and physical) existed, but were not perfectly united. In some Gnostic treatises, it is not the divine Savior who dies on the cross, but another who dies in his place. In still other treatises, the heavenly man merely came upon an earthly body, but left that body prior to the crucifixion (Second Treatise of Seth VII 51:20—52:3 NHL 330; VII 56:8-11 NHL 332).

While the secessionists may have held beliefs that lent themselves to Gnostic interpretation, it is doubtful that they ought to be called Gnostic.

The beliefs of the secessionists, as reconstructed from the epistles of John, seem neither as fully developed as nor entirely congruent with Gnostic systems developed in later writings. But it is probable that the kinds of beliefs they held fed into the stream of thought known as Gnosticism.

In summary, while striking parallels can be adduced between early known heresies and the epistles of John, none of these heresies perfectly mirrors the false teaching of 1 and 2 John. Yet the options outlined above do show that already in the early days of the church there were varying theories about the human nature of Jesus, about the union of divine and human in him and about his suffering and death. We also see a tendency to deny or minimize the humanity of Jesus. Whatever the heresy may have been which these dissidents advocated, they would not have labeled it by any of these names or agreed that it was heresy. Surely they would have regarded themselves as "Christians" insofar as that name means followers of Jesus Christ! The problem facing the Elder and his congregations is thus complicated by the subtlety of the heresy and the avowed sincerity of its proponents.

The Purpose and Genre of 1 and 2 John The main purpose of these two epistles is to combat a tangle of erroneous teaching and practice. Second John is a real letter, written to a specific congregation, to warn it that false teachers might come their way, to remind the faithful of the teaching that they had been given and to urge them to cherish the bonds of love that bind them together as a Christian fellowship. By contrast, 1 John lacks the features that characterize genuine correspondence, and has been variously called a treatise, sermon, tract or pastoral manual. Yet, like Paul's letters, 1 John is intended for a specific audience and directed to a particular situation. It is possible that 1 John was sent to more than one congregation; some have suggested it was originally written (and read aloud) in smaller segments to a congregation in the author's vicinity or to which he belonged.

First John is also permeated by a gentle pastoral tone. The author desires to encourage his readers and to assure them of their standing as God's children. The turmoil within their congregation undoubtedly caused many to question their own faith and practice, and to wonder whether they were also guilty of or prone to the failings of the departed dissidents. First John regularly reassures its readers of those things in which they can have confidence. But at the same time it urges them to continue in faithfulness to the God who has given them so much.

B. The Occasion and Purpose of 3 John Third John fits broadly into the same setting and milieu as 1 and 2 John, but it does not seem to deal with the identical issues. It is a personal letter, addressed to Gaius, and has three main purposes: first, to commend Gaius and his practice of welcoming traveling missionaries into his home; second, to express disapproval of the conduct of Diotrephes, who refuses to welcome these same missionaries; third, to commend one of these itinerant ministers, Demetrius, to Gaius and to urge that he be received with hospitality. In fact, 3 John may be a letter of commendation that Demetrius carried. The apostle Paul refers to such letters in passing (2 Cor 3:1-3).

Beyond this, it is difficult to pinpoint the nature of the problem in 3 John. The letter does not address the problems of heresy and schism evident in 1 and 2 John. Although some commentators have suggested that Diotrephes may well be one of the dissident former church members—for this would explain his refusal to receive any itinerant prophets from the Elder—others point out that the Elder does not allude to any doctrinal deviation on Diotrephes' part, nor to his defection from the community. If either of these had been known to the Elder, he surely would have referred to them. It is, therefore, more likely that the dispute between Diotrephes and the Elder rests on other grounds.

We might call the dispute a power struggle. Some commentators have noted that the Elder cannot peremptorily dismiss Diotrephes. The Elder would like to visit the church so that he can "call attention to what [Diotrephes] is doing" (3 Jn 10). This kind of language suggests that the Elder has legitimate authority in the congregation, but perhaps his authority comes not by virtue of an appointed office, but through familiarity with and seniority in the church. At any rate, Diotrephes has challenged his position, for what reasons we can only guess. The Elder merely states that Diotrephes "loves to be first." Yet other issues may have been at stake. Even if Diotrephes felt that he was exercising legitimate authority, he may still have appeared to others simply to be seeking after power.

II. Authorship, Date and Order of the Epistles

Authorship The name of these short letters, "1, 2 and 3 John," comes from the tradition that they were written by the apostle John, the son of Zebedee. The letters themselves are anonymous, although 2 and 3 John state that they are from "the Elder." The similarities in tone, language, thought and situation are such that we may safely conjecture that all three letters come from the same pen. But was that author, the "Elder," the apostle John?

There are two kinds of evidence for assigning the epistles to the apostle John. First, evidence is taken from the epistles themselves. Some statements within the epistles suggest that they were written by an eye-witness of Jesus' ministry (1 Jn 1:1-4). However, while firsthand testimony fits with a theory of apostolic authorship, it does not necessarily demand it. After all, there were other eyewitnesses to Jesus' ministry; and Paul speaks of five hundred who were witnesses to the resurrection.

Other evidence derives from early church tradition, according to which the epistles were written by John, the son of Zebedee, one of the twelve disciples of Jesus (see Brown 1984:9-13). Apparently the apostles were called "presbyters" or "Elders" (compare Eusebius, *Ecclesiastical History* 3.39.4.), but other leaders in the early church were granted this honorific designation as well. Eusebius quotes Papias (ca. 60-130), who refers to an "Elder John," but it is debated whether he is the same person as an earlier named John, who was one of the Twelve (see Stott 1988:39-44; Marshall 1978:42-48).

Of course the lack of unambiguous evidence for the apostolic authorship of the epistles does not disprove their apostolic origins, but neither does it settle the question. The possibility of apostolic authorship should not be discounted, but in view of the ambiguous evidence, exegetical decisions and interpretation should not be based on an a priori assumption of such authorship. With this disclaimer in mind, there is no reason not to designate the author of the epistles by his traditional name, "John."

Date Typically the epistles are assigned to the end of the first century, perhaps somewhere between the years A.D. 90 to 100. One of the chief reasons for dating the letters late in the first century is their relationship to the Gospel of John, which is usually dated between the years A.D. 70

to 100. If the epistles were written after the Gospel, as most scholars assume, then they must fall in the last decade or so of the first century.

Order Questions of authorship and date raise two other related questions—those of the relationship between the Gospels and epistles, and of the order in which the epistles themselves were written. Clearly there is a relationship between the Gospel of John and the epistles of John, for the language, theology and situations are closely related. But the epistles are written after the Gospel, within the same general milieu, to deal with a new set of problems that has arisen within the church.

The order in which the epistles were written is more difficult to discern. We may hypothesize that 1 John was written to deal pastorally and theologically with the crisis confronting the Johannine community. It was both read, in part or in whole, in the congregation of "the Elder," and sent to other congregations that formed the greater "Johannine community." Second John may well have been sent with 1 John as a cover letter to one congregation (or even to several). Third John could have been sent as a cover letter or on its own. Demetrius, who is commended in the letter, may also have carried the letter to a sister church. Perhaps he had a copy of 1 John as well.

III. The Themes of the Epistles

In his refutation of the false teaching, the author appeals to the teaching that the church has had from the beginning (1 Jn 1:1, 5; 2:7, 24; 2 Jn 6, 9); confessional or credal material (1 Jn 2:12-14; 4:2; 5:6); commands given by Jesus (1 Jn 2:7-8); the example of Jesus (2:6; 3:16-17); catechetical instructions (such as 1 Jn 2:1, 7-8, 15-27; 4:4-6; 5:18-20); and the Old Testament (3:11-15). He also appeals to the Holy Spirit's guidance (1 Jn 2:20, 27; 4:1-6, 13-14) and to his readers' personal appropriation of salvation (2:20-21, 27; 3:1-2). In his full-orbed response to the secessionists' false teaching, the Elder touches on numerous points about Christ and salvation.

The Character of God Crucial to these epistles is the author's understanding of the character of God. God is perfectly righteous (1:5, 9; 3:7), faithful (1:9), forgiving (1:9; 2:12), loving (4:7-12, 16, 19), truthful (1:8, 10; 2:20; 4:1-2; 5:20) and pure (1:5, 7; 3:2-3). There is no taint of evil or impurity in God: "God is light; and in [God] there is no darkness at all" (1:5). God's character is manifested in sending Jesus, the Son of God, as the Savior of the world (4:14). By faith in Jesus people are brought into fellowship with God, and hence into fellowship with perfect righteousness, truth, love and purity. Because believers are "born of God," they are given a new life, with a new orientation toward perfect light. Throughout the epistle the author promises believers that they are like God (3:9), assures them that they will be like God (3:1-3) and admonishes them to live in conformity with the character of God (1:7). Here is a call for Christians to center their lives in God.

The Centrality of Jesus Christ Emphasis on the character of God leads naturally to a focus on the centrality of Jesus Christ, for fellowship with God is mediated through the work of God's Son, Jesus. Not surprisingly, the author assumes and emphasizes the unique mediating role of Jesus Christ. The salvation of the children of God has been mediated through the atoning death of Jesus (1:7, 9; 2:1-2), who gave himself— flesh and blood (4:2; 5:6-8)—that those who trust him might live through him (4:9; 5:10-13, 20). The children of God have passed from death to life (3:14) through faith in God's Messiah (2:22-23), the Son of God (2:23-25; 4:9, 13-14; 5:5, 9-12). But as long as they continue in this world, they also continue to depend on his mediating work of atonement and intercession (2:1-2). Salvation is not a status they have attained, but a gift they receive.

Christian Discipleship While Christians are intimately related to God as God's children, they await a future "appearing" of Christ to complete the work begun at his first appearing (2:28—3:3). When Jesus appears, they shall indeed be transformed into the likeness of God (3:2); but they have not yet attained that status. Salvation is not only a present possession, but a future hope as well. In the meantime, the preferred image for the Christian life in this epistle is that of the path or of "walking," an image that comes from the pages of the Old Testament and is found often in the Psalms and Proverbs. The image of discipleship as "walking" in a certain way suggests not a plateau that one achieves, but a manner and style of life to which one is committed.

Moreover, Jesus himself provides the definition and example of righteousness that the children of God are to emulate (2:6; 3:16-17). The Incarnate Word of God died that they might live, but his life exemplified the obedience and love that they are to manifest as well. Salvation is not a purely internal, private or individual communion with God. Fellowship with and knowledge of God come to expression in conduct, and the Johannine epistles stress the practical, visible and concrete manifestation of one's commitments in everyday life. If one is committed to the Jesus who died on the cross, then one must express that commitment in similar self-giving love (1 Jn 3:16). Commitment to a righteous God demands righteousness in life (2:6; 3:4-10). Love of God is impossible without love of others (4:7-8, 16, 20-21).

In this regard, note that the word *truth* in Johannine theology does not refer only to doctrine or belief. It also covers the way one lives: truth always includes orthodoxy (correct belief) and orthopraxy (correct practice). Neither has precedence over the other, for *truth is always both belief and practice*. One cannot know the truth and fail to do the truth; one cannot do the truth without knowing it. This is a far richer and more integrated view of the Christian life than many Christians hold.

Love, Unity and Fellowship The schism that this church has experienced is not understood simply as an unfortunate but unavoidable division. The departure of the dissidents repeats Judas' defection from the circle of disciples. They have abandoned the sphere of life and light for death and darkness; they have broken Jesus' command to love each other as he loved them (Jn 13:34); they have mocked the purpose of his death: to gather together "one flock" under "one shepherd" (Jn 10:16).

Some of the most-quoted statements from 1 John are surely those about God's love. Simple yet sublime affirmations such as "God is love" are hard to improve on or to paraphrase. A key verse is 1 John 4:19, "We love because [God] first loved us." Here we are to take the "because" quite literally. Christian love for each other grows from God's prior love. Our ability to love depends on the power of God's love in us, enabling us to love others.

From the human angle, the love of which John writes is clearly more than emotion, sentiment or affection, although it may have elements of each of those within it. Rather, love is commitment. The concern of the epistles is to whom and to what our loves are directed. Here we may take the admonition "Do not love the world, or the things of the world" (2:15) as key. Christians are not to allow the world to shape their lives, but to love God and allow that love to direct all that they are and do.

The Preservation of Sound Teaching The teaching to which the epistles urge their readers to be faithful is teaching that they understand to be the tradition of the community. In Protestant circles, "tradition" is not a particularly popular or important concept. The sense in which tradition is used here, however, is in its technical sense: *tradere* means to pass on, and tradition is that which is passed on, beginning with the eyewitnesses and continuing as a chain of witnesses in which each succeeding generation forms a link. First John in particular calls its readers to affirm and hold on to "that which was from the beginning" (1:1), the "old command" (2:7), the message that had been declared to them (1:5). The challenge for the church is to cast its teaching in ways that are at once faithful to the message that has been handed on to it and that communicates to the cultures to which they minister. Such contextualization is always fraught with peril. But an unacceptable alternative is merely to repeat Christian jargon or the words of Scripture. Mere repetition, even of the Scriptures, does not guarantee understanding of or fidelity to them.

The Importance of Discernment Discernment is a theme that runs throughout 1 John, even though it is directly addressed in one section only (4:1-6). Discernment is the ability to distinguish truth from error, whether that truth be manifested in doctrine or practice. While the gift of discernment comes from the Holy Spirit, it is not confined to the individual or to inner experience. Discernment is the task of the community. The church as a corporate entity is to guard, preserve and nurture truth. Indeed, in a church that so stresses the need for love and unity, it would be strange if at the point of discerning the truth the author would suddenly appeal to the private individual, without casting an eye on the community at large. This community has two primary manifestations: the community that has gone before us, and the community in which we now fellowship. The church is to test the spirits to see whether they conform with that which has been carefully taught and safeguarded by the church in the past, in order to preserve the continuity and life of the church today.

Assurance and Confidence One theme that permeates 1 John in particular is the theme of assurance. Again and again the author assures his readers that they can be confident of their standing with God. Believers are the children of God (3:1-3), born of God, with new life. Believers have assurance of salvation because they trust in the God who gives salvation, new birth and new life. God keeps them in eternal life; it is not earned by one's own efforts or superior moral achievements. Those who make it their aim to "walk in the light" and recognize their need for the forgiveness of God when they fail do not need to be anxious about God's graciousness to them. God is "faithful and just to forgive us our sins," for "God is love." Assurance rests on what God does and has done for those who trust in God.

IV. Learning to Read and Apply the Epistles of John

The Importance of Historical Context In interpreting any book of Scripture, the more we know about the historical setting of the material, the better we can interpret it. One of the things that we can glean from the epistle is that the church to which the elder has written has been torn apart by schism. In order to interpret 1 John, it is important always to keep this setting in mind. We can illustrate how important this historical setting is with a brief illustration.

Take, for example, the statements in 1 John 2:3-4, "We can be sure we know him if we obey his commands. The [one] who says, 'I know [God],' but does not do what he commands is a liar, and the truth is not in him." If we interpret these statements without any attention to historical context, then the verses seem to mean that *anyone* who claims to know God—which would include most Christians—but who breaks one of God's commands is a liar, and does not know God or have God's indwelling truth. This would exclude most, if not all, Christians from "knowing God"!

However, it is instructive to remember that there has been a split in the church, and that the dissident faction has broken the commands to believe in Jesus and to love the children of God (see 1 Jn 3:23). When John speaks of "the [one] who says, 'I know him' " but fails to keep God's commands, John is referring to one of these secessionists. That is, he is applying a principle accepted by himself and the community to a specific situation. The general principle is that those who know God also do what God commands. When someone consistently disobeys the commands of God, then that person's claim to know and serve God is also called into question. John has not formulated a test to apply to individual or isolated acts of faithful believers, but to the lifestyle of a group of people that has left the church. He is not looking so much at specific acts or individual persons as he is at a conception of the Christian life with which he disagrees.

In short, whenever the author speaks of people who are not doing something they ought to be doing—like loving, believing or keeping the commands—he is directing his remarks not so much to Christians in his churches who are doing these things imperfectly, but to the secessionists who are not doing them at all. These letters were not intended primarily to whip believers into shape or to serve as warnings to the faithful, so much as they were to encourage them that the path in which they were walking was indeed the path of God's will. When John speaks of those who are not doing what God requires, his mind is on the secessionists. Most, if not all, of the warnings are directed to those who have left the community and abandoned the apostolic teaching.

To apply these epistles today, a pastor or teacher must discern when a congregation or individual needs encouragement and when they need exhortation. Passages that were originally intended to be applied to the secessionists cannot simply be applied to those who have been and continue to be faithful to the apostolic message. But just because John encourages his congregation and believes that they are walking as God would have them to walk does not mean that exhortations to love, obedience and confession are not appropriate for the church today. Today the epistles sound the same call as they did in the first century— to bring all of one's life under the scrutiny of God's light, and to live in conformity with God's character and will.

The Importance of Literary Context It is also important to interpret individual passages by setting them within the context of the epistles as a whole. One example may suffice here. The statement "everyone who loves has been born of God and knows God" (1 Jn 4:7), when interpreted without reference to context, could be construed to mean that love is the evidence that one stands in relationship to God. But elsewhere in the epistle, belief in Jesus is advanced as the test of one's relationship to God (5:1). And, similarly, keeping the commandments is likewise taken as evidence that one "lives in [God]" (3:24).

In context, each of these verses is making a specific point. Here, for example, the point is that love for others must characterize those who love God. But love is not the only characteristic of those who love God. Indeed, the epistle might well be read as a series of short sermons, in which various aspects of the Christian life—belief, love, conduct, obedience, discernment or confession—are examined. In interpreting the epistles one should press beyond the surface statements to ask how they cohere with each other, as well as what the fundamental and basic understanding of God and the Christian life is that they manifest. The letter's simplicity lends itself to simplistic interpretation; to the attuned ear, however, its commands are calls to understand and live in light of the nature and character of God.

Dualism Perhaps one of the most puzzling features of Johannine thought is its adamant dualism. "Dualism" is, as its name implies, the view that the world is divided into two opposing and conflicting realities, such as matter and spirit. Johannine dualism sets life and death, love and hate, truth and error, light and darkness, in absolute opposition to each other. Between these opposing realities there is no middle ground. Good is not tinged with evil; truth cannot embrace error; love does not allow room for even a little bit of hate. And yet none of us is perfectly good, loving or truthful. What then are we to make of this dualism?

First, in Johannine dualism the only absolute light, goodness and truth is God (1 Jn 1:5). Divine reality is absolutely unambiguous. Second, believers are in the light because they align themselves with the God who is light, not because they themselves are perfect light. Believers commit themselves to God, to walking in the light, to living according to the standards that flow from the character of God. But they are not absolutely good as God is good. There is no ambiguity in God, but there is ambiguity in every Christian. Third, just as Christians are not unambiguously good, neither is the world absolutely evil or devoid of any truth or goodness. But the "world" consists of those who have not made a commitment to God, who have not given their complete allegiance to the One who is light and life.

In short, Johannine dualism depicts ultimate reality (God) and calls all people to commit themselves to the reality that is truth and light. To make any other choice is not to remain neutral but to elect the only other option, namely, darkness. One need not be completely evil to be on the side of darkness; neither must one be perfectly good to serve the cause of light. But one must make a choice for light. And to choose for light is to choose against darkness.

Two warnings may be issued here with respect to interpreting the dualism of the Johannine world. Although dualism describes the world in clear-cut opposites, such a description should not be taken to mean that we actually see the world in such neat categories. Dualism points to the underlying belief that truth and error, goodness and evil, do not overlap. But in a sinful world, truth and error are not so easy to distinguish, and good and righteousness are not always easy to see or to live out. Moreover, the Elder urges his readers to "test the spirits": such discernment is necessary because the options sometimes come to us in shades of gray. Dualism is a graphic description of the fundamental and ultimate issues of life: that truth, love, life, light and salvation belong to and come from God, while all that is opposed to these realities is also opposed to God. Human beings are faced with the choice to align themselves with one or the other.

This leads us to a second point about applying the dualistic world view. We are exhorted to discern truth from error. We must say, as clearly as possible, of what the truth consists. But it is one thing to pass judgment on ideas, concepts or practices in the abstract; it is quite another to pass judgment on the individuals or people who cherish certain ideas or practices. While we might wish to say quite emphatically that a certain *behavior* comes from and belongs to the darkness, we should feel a certain reticence and humility about making the judgment that a certain *person* belongs to the darkness. Our judgments are always imperfect and incomplete. God, the only perfect judge, alone judges the hearts of people. The church's responsibility is to sound the call to decision, but even more to model that life of righteousness and love to which God calls us. And while the Christian lives constantly with the vision of the absolute dichotomy of truth and falsehood, with the necessity for righteousness and love, putting these things into action is scarcely ever simple. While we can see the general contours of the path of life, that does not mean that each jog in the road or each turn comes clearly marked.

There are still difficult personal and moral decisions to be made, and the choices are not always clear.

Special Problems in Translating the Epistles One recurrent problem in translating and interpreting 1 John especially is the author's use of the pronoun "he" or "him" for God or Jesus. It is sometimes difficult to tell to whom John is referring, and commentators differ on various verses. Based on my interpretation of such passages, I have regularly put [God] or [Jesus] in brackets in order to show to whom I think the author is referring when the reference is ambiguous.

A somewhat related but different problem has to do with the NIV's use of masculine pronouns ("he") and nouns ("brothers") to refer to Christians. It is clear that the epistles do not refer only to men when speaking of those who know God, live in Christ and are to obey the commands, but to all Christians. Moreover, the Greek term translated as "brethren" included "brothers and sisters." Thus, I have rendered these words either in the plural ("they"), with a multiple reference ("brothers and sisters"), or by alternating examples with "she" and "he." I hope that this will help to communicate that the epistles call *all* believers to "walk in the light, as God is in the light" and to live together as brothers and sisters, the children of God.

Outline of 1 John

Outline of 2 John

Outline of 3 John

COMMENTARY

1 John

Through the use of the technologies of telephone, telegraph, computer and satellite, news travels fast. Not so long ago, Southern California was jolted by a rather strong earthquake. Less than fifteen minutes later we heard details about it on a national news program broadcast from Washington, D.C. Meanwhile, in spite of the warnings and pleas of various authorities and officials in the Los Angeles area, telephone lines were jammed as people tried to reach friends and family. In times of crisis and emergency, we instinctively desire to be able to speak to friends and loved ones, especially when we fear that they may have been harmed. We cherish quick and easy communication with others, and we depend upon it to conduct the business of modern life.

During the early years of the spread of the Christian faith, communication between fellow believers and communities of Christians was equally cherished and important. The apostle Paul was able to shepherd his congregations by corresponding with them. But communication was by no means quick and easy. Letters were generally carried by private courier, who traveled on foot, or sometimes by boat or other means.

These journeys were often long and perilous, without the comforts of motels, restaurants, air-conditioned vehicles and paved highways that many of us take for granted when we travel today. And yet for Christians determined to maintain contact with each other, or for church leaders forced to pastor their flocks from afar, the tedious journeys were undertaken despite their risks.

The Character of the Letter We come, then, to a document traditionally known as the First Epistle of John. In its pages we read the words of a pastor concerned about congregations of believers for which he has responsibility, but which lie at some geographical distance from him. Absent from them, yet anxious about them, he pens this short epistle out of his urgent pastoral concern and deep love. He is like the missionary on study leave I met recently, who expressed anxiety and concern for "the family" of believers left behind him.

We assume that 1 John is a letter, even though in many ways it looks more like a treatise, tract or sermon. It lacks the stereotypical forms characteristic of a first-century letter, forms comparable to our salutations ("Dear Friends") and closings ("Warm regards"). By contrast, 2 and 3 John begin as ancient letters should begin, with the identification of the writer (2 Jn 1; 3 Jn 1) and the recipients (2 Jn 2; 3 Jn 1), a greeting (2 Jn 3) and a thanksgiving (2 Jn 4; 3 Jn 2-4). First John, however, does not present itself as a typical letter.

And yet 1 John has the character of a letter insofar as it is directed toward a specific congregation or group of congregations and deals with a particular problem that has arisen. The author assumes familiarity with his readers. He speaks simply in the first person, sometimes in the plural ("we"), sometimes in the singular ("I"; 2:1, 7-8, 12-14, 21, 26; 5:13, 16). He expects his readers to know to whom this "we" or "I" refers, and he writes this epistle expecting his readers to heed it and respond.

The Author as Witness John's authority rests in part on his role as *witness.* The word translated "testify" and "to bear witness" has its roots in the sphere of legal terminology. As in a court of law, witnesses are responsible for the integrity and truthfulness of their testimony (Trites 1978:1049-50). Thus witnesses not only vouch for their personal experience of something, but for the truthfulness of what is stated. The Johannine community cherished those who were "witnesses" to Jesus.

In fact, Jesus himself was viewed as one who bore witness to what he had seen and heard with the Father (Jn 1:18; 5:19, 36; 15:15; compare Rev 1:2, 5; 12:17; 22:20). In turn, the disciples are commissioned as witnesses of Jesus (Jn 15:27). In the epistles we see the continuing role of those who bear witness to Jesus. They do so not only by giving reliable testimony to an event, but also by carrying out the commission to interpret to others the reality of what they had experienced. Witnesses not only tell others what they experienced; they must tell them what it means.

The "witness" in the Johannine churches seems to have had a specific function and role. In many ways, it takes the place of "minister" or "apostle," neither of which is used in a technical sense in the Gospel or epistles of John to refer to preachers of the gospel. But who are these "witnesses"? Are they "eyewitnesses"? In the Gospel and epistles of John the concepts of "seeing" and "sight" can be metaphorical, referring to "insight" and understanding, rather than to literal seeing (compare Jn 1:14; 1 Jn 4:14). For these and other reasons scholars suggest that the "Elder" may not have been an eyewitness, but a follower of one who was an eyewitness. But if he is not an eyewitness, then he is closely tied to one who is, and he is zealous for the preservation of that person's witness. Yet his own testimony is no less important or valid.

☐ Witness to the Word of Life (1:1-4)

Probably each of us has had the experience of speaking in a situation of emergency, under duress or out of anxiety. Our words spill forth, racing ahead of our thoughts, until we run out of breath or someone gently urges us to "slow down." In some ways, the preface of this epistle (1:1-4) points to the urgency of the situation in which the Elder finds himself. His ideas and words tumble forth in his eagerness to express his concerns. Almost awkwardly he repeats himself. Four times he refers to what he has seen or looked at; twice to what he has heard; twice to what he proclaims. But if the wording of the preface is a bit awkward, the author's goal and message is not. Clearly he wishes to underscore that what he is bearing witness to is no figment of his imagination, no invention of his own. He wishes to set before his readers the life that is in Jesus Christ.

The Life Revealed (1:1-2) John's statements are two-pronged. On the one hand, he is stressing that he himself has the credentials of witness: *he* personally experienced that to which he bears witness. But, on the other hand, his role is only that of a witness, of one who points beyond himself to those realities of which he speaks. He does not want to draw attention to himself so much as to the *object* of his experience (Marshall 1978:100), namely, the realities of Jesus' life and ministry. His stance is like that of John the Baptist in the Gospel of John: "[Jesus] must become greater; I must become less important" (Jn 3:30).

Moreover, the role of witness is not limited only to testimony that certain things really happened. A witness also proclaims the meaning and significance of those events. And for John, the significance of what happened in Jesus can be summarized by one word: *life.* Jesus himself is the life of God (1:1) and came to give eternal life to those who believe (1:2).

Thus the message that is proclaimed, *the Word of life,* originates in the words and works of Jesus. Because Jesus was a real human being of flesh and blood, the author can write that *the life appeared; we have seen it and testify to it, and we proclaim to you the eternal life, which was with the Father.* The order of these verbs *(have seen . . . testify . . . proclaim)* is chosen deliberately. They "express in order the three ideas of experience, attestation and evangelism which form part of any genuine and lasting response to the Gospel" (Smalley 1984:9).

The Life Experienced (1:3-4) Because he fulfills these tasks, this author and witness brings subsequent generations into fellowship with God (v. 3). He is one link in a chain of witnesses, stretching from the

---

Notes: **1:1** The object of the verb here consists of four parallel relative clauses. By their placement first in the sentence, the emphasis falls on them. To facilitate comprehension, the NIV introduces the main verb, *we proclaim (apangellomen),* which does not actually appear until verse three, after the dashes.

The antecedent of the neuter pronoun *ho* in the four relative clauses, which together are the object of the verb *proclaim,* is unclear. To be correct grammatically, *ho* (what) cannot refer to *logos,* which is masculine, nor to *zōē* (life), which is feminine; nor ought it to refer to Jesus. Some commentators take the clauses as referring generally to the whole career of the earthly Jesus (Brown 1982:154, 158; Dunn 1980:245; Plummer 1896:14-15), and that is the sense adopted here. Although sometimes in the Johannine writings a neuter pronoun is used when a masculine subject is clearly in view (Jn 3:6; 4:22; 6:37, 39; 17:2, 10; 1 Jn 5:4), there the referent is more easily deduced from the context.

Although the NIV capitalizes *Word* in the phrase *Word of life* and thereby implies that it is Jesus himself, the Incarnate Word, who is in view, this is by no means certain. The personal use of *logos* (word) is found in John only in the prologue (1:1-18). But compare "words of life" in 6:63, which is the message that brings life. For word(s) as "message"

first eyewitnesses to the present day. In that chain, each generation of believers, when it appropriates and testifies to the truth of the gospel, becomes the next link, the next recipient and guardian of that witness. To be sure, both the function and the experience of the eyewitness are distinctive, but they are not thereby superior. Believers—like John's readers and like us today—who have "not seen and yet have believed" (Jn 20:29) are no less in touch with the Word of life who was made manifest.

That life was *with the Father.* This descriptive phrase testifies to both the *origin* and *character* of true life. Life, whether physical or spiritual, is the gift of a gracious, creating, life-giving God. God alone creates and sustains life. And in Jesus, God offers eternal life, which is neither more nor less than knowledge of and fellowship with the one living God (Jn 17:3). God's desire is not to bring death, destruction or condemnation, but life, healing and release. This life can be experienced here and now, for it is received as one becomes a disciple of Jesus Christ. Through the proclamation of the word of life, that is, the message (word) about Jesus (the life), subsequent generations of believers come to know about and ultimately to appropriate life for themselves (compare Jn 4:42). Even as God became visible and tangible in Jesus, so for all subsequent generations of believers, the word of life is that visible and tangible witness to Jesus (Culpepper 1985:7).

Because the message that is proclaimed serves to mediate knowledge of and fellowship *with the Father and with his Son, Jesus Christ,* John

---

compare John 4:41; 5:24, 38, 47; 8:31, 37, 47, 51-52, 55; 12:48; 14:10; 17:8. *Word* is best taken as meaning message or proclamation (Barker 1981:306; Brown 1982:164-65; Bruce 1970:36; Culpepper 1985:8-9; Dodd 1946:4-5; Grayston 1984:40; Houlden 1973:50-52; Kysar 1986:32; Marshall 1978:103; Stott 1988:72-75). Some scholars suggest that the author plays on both Gospel meanings of *word* (Houlden 1973:52; Marshall 1978:103; Smalley 1984:6-7; Smith 1991:36), a suggestion sometimes coupled with or dependent on the view that the preface of the epistle is modeled on the Gospel's prologue (so Houlden 1973:46 and Brown 1982:178; Grayston 1984:40-41 argues just the reverse).

Word of life is taken here as an objective genitive (the word about life). The force of *ap' archēs (from the beginning)* in the epistle is to stress the unchanging nature of whatever is in view in the context. As a paraphrase for *from the beginning,* Dodd (1946:5, and n. 1) aptly suggests "what has always been true about [the Gospel]." *From the beginning* echoes John 1:1 (and Gen 1:1), but refers to the beginning of Jesus' ministry or the message preached about it (Houlden 1973:49; Bruce 1970:35; Dunn 1980:245; Grayston 1984:37-38). Smith (1991:36) suggests that it refers specifically to the Incarnation.

finds it necessary to stress that this message has not changed. The truth has been the same *from the beginning.* The word was the truthful message that was proclaimed by Jesus, heard by the eyewitnesses and now handed on to subsequent generations (1:1, 5; 2:6-7). The warning to the church is implicit: "The baton is being passed to you—don't drop it!"

Apparently the message has been changed in unacceptable ways by some members of the congregation, to the extent that the message they preach no longer can be called the word of life. And those who do not adhere to the *Word of life* cannot have true fellowship together with those who do. For ultimately the fellowship that believers share together is not simply that of an accidental conglomeration of people with some things in common. Rather, what believers in Christ have in common is fellowship with God. Those who know and love God are joined to each other as well.

For the author of 1 John, then, failing to confess the true message has dire consequences. Failure to hold to what is true means that one can have fellowship neither with the faithful nor with God. But how is right belief the basis for fellowship? Does John really mean to assert that fellowship with other believers and with God depends on the correctness of all one's beliefs? We do well to remember that the epistle contends for the most fundamental of all religious beliefs, namely, belief in God. More specifically, what is at issue is the relationship of the Father and the Son (v. 3) and, hence, the way in which one comes to know God. If it is not the God made known in Jesus Christ in whom we place our trust, then fellowship is with some other god (5:21) and not with the God who has always been proclaimed *(from the beginning).*

This implies, in turn, that there is no true *fellowship* with those who do not hold the same confession about the Father and Son. *Fellowship* literally means "sharing in common." Where people deny the basic con-

---

1:2-4 Sometimes in the epistle the author uses the first-person plural to include himself with all Christians (see 1:9; 3:1; 4:10), and sometimes the pronoun refers exclusively to himself, either as an editorial "we," or as a genuine plural (1:3, 5). When "we" is taken in the exclusive sense, to whom does it refer? It may refer to the author and others who were eyewitnesses to the ministry of Jesus and who subsequently wrote to some (the "you") who were not (Bruce 1970:35-38; Marshall 1978:106-7; Stott 1988:66-68). Other commentators argue that the first-person plural means "the Church in solidarity with eyewitnesses" (Smalley 1984:8; Dodd 1946:9-16; Houlden 1973:48, 53). Brown (1982:160) refers it to "the

fessions about God that the word of the gospel affirms, friendship or meaningful relationship can exist. But there cannot be Christian fellowship such as John envisions it. Fellowship is the unity of those who have appropriated the life granted to them by God. The shared experience of life in Jesus alone constitutes true Christian fellowship.

Christian fellowship is and ought to be characterized by joy—a joy that John describes as "complete" or "fulfilled" (Jn 3:29; 15:11; 16:24; 17:13; 2 Jn 4, 12; 3 Jn 4). Here John writes that his joy will be completed when his readers heed his words and continue in fellowship with him and with God. Joy is given through and rests on this fellowship. Like the psalmist, who proclaims "you will fill me with joy in your presence, with eternal pleasures at your right hand" (Ps 16:11), John describes joy as a gift of God, which comes from the knowledge and experience of the life that God gives.

Biblical writers continually looked for the day when they would know joy, when they would rejoice. But John writes in this epistle that the expected joy of fellowship with God is now available to those who fellowship with God through Jesus. No need to wait any longer—full joy can be ours through Jesus Christ. A long-awaited blessing of the messianic age is here. Joy is not given to us apart from the circumstances of our earthly life, or as a substitute for pain or an escape from sorrow. Joy does not depend upon the elimination of the things that weigh us down or trouble us here. Joy comes from the deep trust of knowing that precisely in this world one is nevertheless in touch with the God who has given us life in the midst of the death that surrounds us. So with the psalmist the author of the epistle would gladly say that there is joy in the presence of God. We have joy now as we experience God's presence in Jesus. Sharing together God's presence, God's gift of life, completes our joy.

---

tradition-bearers and interpreters who stand in a special relationship to the Beloved Disciple in their attempt to preserve his witness" (compare Culpepper 1985:8). On any reading, both eyewitness testimony and its preservation by subsequent generations are important in preserving the word of life; hence the author's anxiety about his readers' faithfulness (Houlden 1973:53; Culpepper 1985:8).

1:3 Moule (1959:165; compare Plummer 1896:19; Smalley 1984:12) suggests the force of the *kai . . . de* in verse 3 may be rendered by "moreover" or, "Yes, and our fellowship is with the Father."

□ Walking in the Light: The Fundamental Pattern (1:5—2:27)

What does God want of me? What does God want of us? Probably every Christian has asked these very questions. They are asked in times of anguish, during crisis and decision making and, implicitly and explicitly, on a day-to-day basis. What does God require of those who want to offer their sincere allegiance and devotion?

The next section of 1 John (1:5—2:27) tackles this question, for the church to which John was writing debated this very issue. What does God ask of us? What does it mean to be a disciple of Jesus? What does it mean to be a faithful Christian? To address this issue, John uses the image of "walking in the light." And he lays out certain expectations of those who desire to *walk in the light*. We can summarize these expectations briefly: imitation of God's character (1:5-7); dependence upon the cleansing from sin provided by Jesus' death (1:7, 9; 2:1-2); obedience to the commands of God (2:3-6), especially the command to love (2:7-11); and steadfast resistance to the lure of the ways of the world (2:15-17) and to false teaching (2:18-27).

So, if we do all these things, are we then doing what God wants? Are we walking in the light? We cannot simply mark these things off on a checklist. For there is a unifying thread woven through the pattern of "walking in the light." These "expectations" are unified by an understanding of God's character and of God's activity in Christ. Thus John begins with an assertion about God, the simple statement that *God is light*. Everything depends upon and flows from that statement. It is worth examining at some length.

The Character of God (1:5) In many ways the statement that *God is light* is the thesis of the epistle. It includes a definition of God's character as well as implications for the life of Christian discipleship. In

---

Notes: 1:5 Nowhere else in the New Testament does the word *message* refer to the gospel, for which the usual designation is *euangelion*. But that word does not appear in the Johannine literature. *Angelion* is virtually synonymous with "the Word of life" (1:2).

From him (ap' autou) could refer to God or to Jesus, but the reference to eyewitness testimony in 1:1-4 suggests that Jesus' proclamation is in view. The *we* still refers to the authoritative interpreters of the tradition of Jesus' words and ministry, and the *you* to those who heard it from the Elder and other preachers.

In the phrase *no darkness at all* the words rendered *no* and *at all* translate two Greek

fact, to lay bare the relationship between the character of God as light and Christian life as "walking in the light" is the whole point of the first part of the epistle.

God is light is not a particularly startling statement. Indeed, this assertion would be at home in many of the world's religions, including those within the orbit of John's first-century world (compare Grayston 1984:46-47). Who would quarrel with depicting the Deity, the greatest power and greatest good in the world, with the symbol of light? In fact, John may have used the word deliberately, aware of both the simple power of the statement and its broad appeal.

But we should also remember the Old Testament imagery to which John appeals. We can summarize the references to light in the Old Testament under three main headings. First, light attends and characterizes *God's self-manifestation* (Ex 3:1-6; 13:21-22; Ps 104:4). The psalmist pictures God clothed in garments of light (Ps 104:2; compare 1 Tim 6:16), an appropriate symbol for the One who is pure, righteous and holy. Second, *God's revelation* through the spoken and written word gives light. That word offers moral guidance and direction for living in accordance with God's will. Often quoted in this connection are verses from the Psalms: "Thy word is a lamp to my feet and a light to my path" (Ps 119:105, 130; 43:3; 56:13; Prov 6:23; Job 24:13; 29:3; Is 2:5; Dan 5:11, 14). Just as light shows people where to walk when it is dark, so God shows the way in which human beings are to walk: "in your light we see light" (Ps 36:9). Third, light symbolizes *God's salvation.* The psalmist celebrates God who is "my light and my salvation" (27:1; 18:28), and light is a favorite image of the prophet Isaiah to depict God's saving activity on behalf of the people of God (9:1; 58:8, 10; 60:1, 19-20).

These images are of course related: as light shows the way in darkness, so also by virtue of God's revelation are we able to know God and the

---

negatives *(ouk . . . oudemia),* an emphatic negation, with the emphasis on the last part of the sentence.

The phrase *put the truth into practice* (Gk *poiein tēn alētheian*) is found in the Old Testament (Neh 9:33) but is paralleled more closely in Jewish texts from 200 B.C. to A.D. 200, such as the Qumran Scrolls, the Testaments of the Twelve Patriarchs, and the apocryphal book of Tobit, where it has the meaning of living in accord with the truth. Doing things that are evil (see Jn 3:20) and doing what is sinful (see 1 Jn 3:4, 8-9) are its opposite.

path in which we are to walk, a path that leads to God. To have knowledge of God and to walk in the way that God requires constitutes salvation. And this is the message, the word of eternal life (1:1), which the author of the epistle has heard and declares (v. 5). The Elder takes particular pains to note that it comes ultimately from Jesus (*from him;* compare 1:1, "that which was from the beginning"), even if the exact form of these words cannot be found recorded in any one Gospel (compare Jn 8:12; 9:5; 17:3). But the work and words of Jesus were testimonies to the God who is light.

Lest there be any misunderstanding, John emphatically restates the point: *in him there is no darkness at all.* God is pure light, not diluted or mixed in any way with evil, hatred, untruth, ignorance or hostility. *God is light* is not a theoretical assertion about the nature of God, but a statement that drives us to the heart of what God is like. God is pure light, and for John this statement rings with implications for the Christian life. Thus it is crucial that we correctly grasp this basic truth.

Now, if we agree that God is pure light, how does it help us answer the question, What does God want of us? John's answer comes here in absolute terms: light and darkness are as incompatible in the Christian as they are in God (see the discussion of dualism in the introduction). We can picture this with two circles. One contains in it truth (1:6, 8; 2:21), love (3:1; 4:7-12), righteousness (1:9; 2:1, 29; 3:7), eternal life (1:2; 2:17, 25), hope (3:3), purity (1:7, 9; 3:3) and confidence (2:28; 3:21; 4:17). This is God's sphere of light, and the children of light walk in it. In biblical thought *walking* (1:6-7) is a synonym for living (Prov 6:23; Ps 1). Thus to say that Christians *walk in the light* is another way of saying that Christian life is lived within the circle of God's light. In it we catch a vision of God, and we are able to discern and follow the way of righteousness and truth that is salvation and life. C. S. Lewis put it this way: "We believe that the sun is in the sky at midday in summer not because we can clearly see the sun (in fact, we cannot) but because we can see everything else" (Lewis 1947:133). We cannot see the light; but by and in the light we see everything else.

Alongside this circle lies another that circumscribes all that is antithetical to the goodness of light. In this circle are falsehood (1:6, 8), hatred (1:9; 3:13, 15; 4:20), impurity (1:7, 9), fear (4:18) and sinfulness (2:16).

This is the sphere of evil, what is called the "world" (2:15-17; 3:3) and "darkness" (1:6; 2:6, 8). It consists of all that God is not and is inimical to God and the circle of light.

These two circles share nothing in common. They do not overlap at all. God has no fellowship with darkness, for God is pure light. God is wholly righteous. And the children of God are to walk in the light and not in darkness. To *walk in the light* means to shape one's whole being, all one's actions, decisions, thoughts and beliefs by the standard of the God who is light, even as a circle gives shape to empty space. It does not mean to be perfect, as God is perfect, for the author's statements about human sinfulness (1:8, 10) do not allow such an interpretation. Rather, to *walk in the light* means to live continually guided by and committed to the God who is light. What God wants of us is that we shape our lives not by an external norm or by some arbitrary standard, but in conformity with the very character and heart of God.

And here is where the image of the circle is helpful. Prior to drawing a circle on paper, there is only blank space. But a circle includes and excludes space, just as the circle of God's light includes and excludes certain actions and behaviors. The circle gives shape to space, and so serves as a boundary. And, indeed, the most obvious feature of a circle is this outer boundary. But circles themselves are not defined or constructed from their edges, but from a fixed and known center. So to understand the boundary of the circle of God's light, we do well to focus on the center, not on the edges. The commitment that John seeks, that we *walk in the light,* consists of focusing ever more closely on the center of the circle of light, which is God, and learning to live in conformity with that center. Where there is no center, the edges blur and fade away. Where there is a living center, the boundaries need not be a matter of constant worry and concern.

Here is where we might be tempted to quit, to give up or to say, "If that's what God wants, that leaves me out. I can't ever be like God." But the Elder is not yet through with his discussion about what it means to follow the God who is light. In the next section, he has to deal with the problem of human sinfulness. If Christians can become light, as God is light, then they need to know how to do so. But John seems to assume that this is not the ideal or goal. We are to walk in the light; we are never told to *be* light. And yet some people in John's church may have made just this assumption: If God is light, then aren't we also light as well? The next section explains how *not* to understand the assertion *God is light*. It also offers encouragement to those who might feel that just as God's ways are not our ways, so in this life God's character can never be completely ours.

The Atonement of Christ (1:6—2:2) These verses contain six if-clauses. Three of them (vv. 6, 8, 10) are claims that the author views as false deductions to draw from the belief that *God is light*. These claims may be slogans or summaries of the position of the dissidents who have left the fellowship. Apparently each claim is based on the assumption that if God is perfect light, then those who are God's children are perfect light as well. While the secessionists may echo the author's teaching, they distort it at crucial points.

Although John speaks in the first person plural ("we"), this does not necessarily imply that any of his readers, those who have remained faithful, are actually making such claims. Rather, he is using a rhetorical device to make vivid the danger of adopting this viewpoint: "Now imagine if we were to say. . . ." To each of these false statements, then, John advances a theological counterclaim (1:7, 9; 2:1). Each counterclaim consists of two parts: first, he refutes the secessionists' claim to be without sin, to be light as *God is light;* second, he affirms the importance of the atoning work of Christ for the sinner. Indeed, these two are integrally related, for to deny one's sin is ultimately to deny the need for Christ's atonement.

The Incompatibility of Light and Darkness (1:6-7) But let us make no mistake. The Elder will let no one off the hook who thinks that somehow, within the Christian, light and dark may safely and happily coexist. Light and darkness are opposites, and repel each other. One cannot have fellowship with God with one foot in darkness and one in light, since *God is light; in him there is no darkness at all.* One cannot serve God, who is light, while continuing to dwell in the realm that is hostile to or ignorant of God, which is the realm of darkness, for that is both to deny the very nature of God as pure light and to deny that God's character ought to shape ours as well.

Here it is crucial to take note of what the author does *not* say. "Darkness" is not simply equivalent to sin or wrongdoing. It is the realm that opposes and is hostile to God. This realm is characterized by disobedience and lack of relationship to God. Thus John exhorts Christians—and all people—not to walk in darkness. But notice that he never says "Let there be no darkness in you," as if he were saying, "True Christians are without a trace of sin." *Darkness* is not a synonym for "indwelling sin." Darkness and light are not realities that are *within* each of us. Rather, they are realities greater than and external to us. Darkness and light are two opposing forces, each making their competing claims upon us. We are challenged to decide in which circle we will choose to live, and then we endeavor to live within it. This is to *live by the truth.*

There are many synonyms for the expression *live by the truth:* "does the will of God" (2:17), "do what pleases [God]" (3:22) and "does what is right" (2:29; 3:7; compare 3:10). Although the phrase aims at concrete moral and practical actions, it means more than "practicing what we preach." It means living in conformity with truth and light, living in accord with the character of God. Those whose allegiance is truly to God will be shaped by that commitment and by God's own character.

The result of committing oneself to God and to *walk in the light* is twofold. First, we have fellowship *with one another.* Those in the light are joined together in a fellowship whose primary guiding principle is Jesus' own command of mutual love (2:7-11). Second, those in this fellowship can be assured that *the blood of Jesus, his Son, purifies us from every sin* ("all sin"). In other words, those in the light do indeed sin—but they recognize the need to be purified from sin. On the other hand, those who claim they can walk in darkness deny the need for purification. At first glance, this may strike us as an anomaly. Even though sin appears to belong in the realm of darkness, the continued intention to *walk in the light* and to shape one's life by God's own character will itself lead to a recognition of what is false and impure in us. We understand that impure actions or attitudes cannot simply be tolerated or ignored. We understand the implications of what it means that "God is light." But we also understand that we are not perfect light as God is. And yet we can also be confident that the *blood* or death of Jesus serves to wash away the impurity so that the believer may continue in fellowship with God (compare 1:3, 6; 2:3). And this acceptance of Jesus' death on our behalf is an ongoing part of our own walking in the light.

Fellowship with God is not mystical communion with a vague divine entity but a commitment to a righteous God, a commitment that in turn lays the demand upon us to *walk in the light*. Against the secessionists, then, the author asserts that not every experience which is claimed as an experience of God is in fact fellowship with God. Fellowship with God will always be characterized by walking in the light, doing the truth, living as God desires.

The Necessity of Confession (1:8-9) The recognition of what is impure and false in us ought to lead us to confess our sins. A few years ago an article entitled "Pick-and-Choose Christianity" appeared in a major national magazine. This article summarized the results of a three-year study of Christians of all denominations in a midwestern state, pointing out that most church members "pick and choose" which of the teachings of Christianity they will accept and which they will leave behind. One of the least popular teachings was that regarding sin. The article stated,

> What many have left behind is a pervasive sense of sin. Although 98% said they believe in personal sin, only 57% accepted the traditional notion that all people are sinful and fully one-third allowed that they "make many mistakes but are not sinful themselves." Said one typical respondent: "The day I die, I should only have to look up at my Maker and say, 'Take me.' Not 'Forgive me.' "

No doubt there are many reasons for the loss of a consciousness of sin, but the phenomenon is scarcely new or endemic to the United States in the twentieth century. First John reflects a similar situation, for apparently some people in the church were claiming to be without sin. How could such a claim have arisen? It seems that some people had taken the belief that God is light and therefore irrevocably set against darkness and drawn an extreme conclusion: If God is indeed light—and here they would agree with the Elder—it follows that those who are God's children (3:1-2) are children of light and, hence, are pure and righteous, reflect-

---

1:8 The phrases *to be without sin (hamartian echein)* and *we have not sinned* (v. 10, *hamartanein)* are synonymous (Bultmann 1973:22; Dodd 1946:22-23; Grayston 1984:52; Marshall 1978:114-15). Some scholars, however, think that verse 8 refers to a principle or quality of sin and verse 10 to sinful actions (Brooke 1912:17; Barker 1981:311-13; Smalley 1984:29, 33; Haas 1972:32, 39; Stott 1988:82-84). Thus the dissidents deny that sin has any

ing the character of God. They share God's state of purity. After all, they were "born of God" (2:29; 3:9). What more did they need? As children of God, they had entered into a state that Christians have and cannot lose and that therefore required nothing further of them.

Their claims to sinlessness were strikingly similar to—and probably no less sincere than—those of that American Christian who said, "The day I die, I should only have to look up at my Maker and say, 'Take me.' Not 'Forgive me.' " No one, whether in the first or twentieth century, relishes the thought of labeling one's actions as "sin." Today, in fact, we study the psychology of human actions so that we may better understand their causes and so help to change destructive behaviors. But failure to act with love and justice toward others is still sinful, even if it can be accounted for by our upbringing, some event in our past or an unhappy relationship or experience. However much we can provide explanations or rationalizations for sin, they do not excuse it.

The author answers his opponents' claim to be sinless by asserting that they are self-deceived. They are not merely confused, but deceived by the greatest lie of all, the lie of the antichrist who opposes Jesus (compare 4:6; 2 Jn 7). Jesus' death would have been pointless were their claims to be sinless true, since his death forgives and purifies believers from their sin and unrighteousness. Although sin appears to put one into darkness, it is actually the claim to be without sin that does so. Confession of sin comes from the truth; denial of sin comes from error. In fact, the very claim to be sinless shows that a lie, and not the truth, is at work within those who make it (compare 1:10, *his word has no place in our lives*). God's truth is not served if we simply cover up the truth about ourselves. God's truth must be manifested in an accurate understanding of God and of ourselves.

Having sent Jesus to cleanse us from sin (v. 7), God remains "faithful and righteous" (NASB; *faithful and just*, NIV) and forgives those who acknowledge their sin. We might have expected to read that God forgives

---

power over them and that they have committed sinful actions. Yet a third view is that verse 8 refers to the guilt incurred by sin and verse 10 to acts of sin (Brown 1982:204-5, 211-12).

1:9 The NIV obscures a possible play on words here: God who is righteous (NIV, *just; dikaios)* cleanses human beings from their unrighteousness *(adikia)*.

out of love or mercy and punishes due to justice. But John calls on the Old Testament concept of God's steadfastness to the covenant that has been established by using familiar descriptions of God as one who does what is *faithful and just* (compare Deut 32:4; Jer 42:5). Despite our unrighteousness *(adikia)*, God is righteous *(dikaios)* and sends one to us who is also righteous (2:1). By depending upon the work of Jesus, who is righteous, we are able to continue to walk in fellowship with one who is light.

The Intercession of Jesus Christ (1:10—2:2) Once again we read the claim to be without sin. This time the author levels his most serious charge yet: those who claim to be without sin *make [God] out to be a liar*. In fact their claim shows that it is not God's word or God's message *(logos; 1:1, 5)* that they have received, but quite another message. We have then a crescendo of charges: "It is one thing knowingly to tell an untruth or lie; it is worse to deceive oneself to the point where there is no truth; it is still worse to make God a liar" (Brown 1982:231). The denial of sin makes God a liar because it rejects God's provision for sin, the *atoning sacrifice* of Jesus Christ.

Although John's purpose in writing is to exhort his readers *so that you will not sin,* he recognizes that people do sin, and that God has established a means of dealing with that sin. Here he introduces the idea of Jesus as an intercessor. Although we are unrighteous, we have an intercessor *(paraklētos)* who is "in the Father's presence" (Brown 1982:216) and who is righteous. A paraclete was an advocate, representative or

---

2:1 There are three words for *children* in the epistles, and one for Son. *Teknia,* the plural of *teknion,* a diminutive, underscores the author's pastoral concern and special relationship to the readers (2:1, 12, 28; 3:7, 18; 4:4; 5:21); *paidia* (2:14, 18), a diminutive of *pais,* is used in direct address to the readers for the sake of variety. For both, compare Proverbs 4:1; 5:1; 7:24; 8:32. *Tekna* is used of Christians as children of God (1 Jn 3:1-2, 10; 5:2) or church members (2 Jn 1, 4, 13; 3 Jn 4) and of unbelievers as "children of the devil" (3:10). Jesus is always called *hyios* in the Johannine literature, a term that is never used of believers. (Compare Brown 1982:213-15; Culpepper 1975:301-2.)

The singular *I write* rather than the plural (1:4, "we write") strikes a more intimate note and is found particularly in passages of exhortation or direct address (2:7; 13-14, 26; see Smalley 1984:35; Brown 1982:215; Haas 1972:40).

Paraclete is found in the New Testament only in the Johannine literature (Jn 14:16-17, 26; 15:26-27; 16:7-11; 1 Jn 2:1). The NIV *one who speaks . . . in our defense* reflects interpretation of the term as a legal assistant or advocate. In the present passage the idea may be that because the exalted Jesus is with God *(pros ton patera),* he intercedes (on the

friend at court who could intercede on one's behalf with the judge. And where the judge is righteous, it is appropriate and to our advantage that the paraclete is righteous as well. Jesus, the righteous one, intercedes with the righteous Father for unrighteous sinners.

But that the risen Christ is an "intercessor with the Father," or, as the NIV renders it, *one who speaks to the Father in our defense,* does not mean that Jesus must plead with an indifferent, reluctant or hardhearted Father on our behalf. Instead, the image of Jesus as intercessor gives us confidence because the penitent believer has as an intercessor the one who has the most intimate relationship with and access to God. Jesus is "with the Father." A vivid example of his intercession is found in John 17, the so-called high priestly prayer in which he prays for the unity and faith of his disciples. Here there is no sense of Jesus trying to persuade God to do something that he requests but that God is reluctant to grant. Such a unity of will exists between Jesus and the Father that Jesus is aware that what he asks will indeed be granted to him. And what he asks for us is forgiveness. It will be granted.

The imagery changes from that of the court to the cultic realm of sacrifice (Balz 1973:169) when John reminds his readers that Christ is also an atonement for sins (NIV, *atoning sacrifice).* Just as Jesus' death has effected purification, cleansing and forgiveness of sin, so now, the Elder asserts, it atones for our sin. It removes sin so that we may continue in fellowship with God. Sin is a blot on the light, and it must be removed. All the images used to speak of Jesus' death remind the readers of this

---

pattern of Old Testament figures such as Abraham and Moses) on our behalf when we pray for forgiveness (1:9), rather than that he enters a plea and defends us in a court of law (Schnackenburg 1963:91; Cullmann 1959:106; Brown 1982:216-17). Similar is the description in Hebrews of the work of Christ on analogy with the High Priest (7:24-28).

The prepositional phrase *pros ton patera* refers to Jesus' present situation; he is "with God" or "in the presence of God" (Bruce 1970:50; Haas 1972:41; Schnackenburg 1963:91; compare 1:2 and Jn 1:1).

In translating the adjective *dikaios* as an appositive and capitalizing it *(the Righteous One),* the NIV renders it as a title (compare Acts 3:14; 7:52; 22:14; 1 Pet 3:18). Jewish literature of the period also testifies to the expectation that the Messiah will be righteous and the messianic era characterized by righteousness (Psalms of Solomon 17:23-52; 1 Enoch 38:2; 53:6). The rabbis developed the thought of the "righteous branch" (Jer 23:5; 33:15; Zech 9:9; compare Longenecker 1970:46-47). However, note that in 1:9 the same adjective is used of God, which the NIV renders *just.*

---

letter that they have fellowship with God on the basis of Christ's work on their behalf. Otherwise they remain in the realm of darkness, impurity and sin. But Christ's death removes the guilt and washes away the impurity that comes from sin.

The imagery of this passage—walking, confessing, purifying—leaves us with a picture of true allegiance to God that is not static but dynamic. John does not picture a plateau that one attains; rather, he envisions a pathway along which we walk. We walk in the light and toward the light. Within that light we know ourselves to be sinners and God to be all righteousness and truth. To know these truths about ourselves and God is the essence of what confession is.

It is said that confession is good for the soul. This is certainly true for the author of our epistle. Here we may conclude by summarizing what confession is and how it is "good for the soul." Confession is, first, the acknowledgment of sin—not the acknowledgment that there is sin, or that sin is wrong, but that "we have sinned against God in thought, word, and deed." Second, then, confession means that we know God as light, as the measure of truth and righteousness by which we fall short. Third, when we confess our sin, we adopt a stance of dependence toward God. Precisely the refusal to confess their sin branded the secessionists as those who scorned the saving work of God on their behalf. Fourth, confession implies a turning to God, a desire to conform ourselves to God's character. Confession does not mean that we say, "I did it again; that's just the way I am." Confession means that we say, "Forgive me, for I have done it again; but I don't want to do it again. Please help me to live within the light of God's truth." Confession is a resource to bring our whole life into conformity with God's will.

Finally, we must always remember that confession is both personal and corporate. In confessing our sins, we acknowledge our place in the company of confessed sinners. Together we stand, on common ground, before God who accepts and forgives all of us. Confession can never be

---

2:2 The meaning of the Greek *hilasmos* (NIV, *atoning sacrifice;* also 4:10) has occasioned no little debate (there is a judicious summary in Brown 1982:217-22). The context suggests "expiation"—that Jesus' death serves to remove our sin, for all the other images in this passage that deal with the purpose of Jesus' death depict the cleansing or removal of sin. Expiation takes "sin" as its object; "propitiation" takes "God" as its object. In this passage (as in 4:10), God's action is directed toward our sins and toward us.

something by which we gain the upper hand over another brother or sister. It certainly is no mark of superiority to confess our sins. It is, rather, simply an acknowledgment of who we are. What God wants of us, then, is sincere commitment to walking in the light and honest confession of our sin.

Obedience to God's Commands (2:3-6) In *The Cost of Discipleship*, Dietrich Bonhoeffer penned the words, "Cheap grace is grace without discipleship, grace without the cross, grace without Jesus Christ, living and incarnate" (1959:47). Cheap grace means living as though God ignores or condones our sins. But forgiveness means that sin is real, and must be dealt with. We cannot ignore it, because God does not ignore it. The denial of sin is not grace: it is a lie. Cheap grace means living without the demand of obedience upon us.

And where there is no call for obedience, then all things are tolerated. "Do your own thing" becomes the motto. And so nothing can be labeled as "sinful." No act is clearly right or wrong. Thus, there is no need of forgiveness. But because John insists that God calls us to obey the commands that have been given, he also reminds us that when we fall short of keeping them, there is forgiveness in Christ. And, to come at it from the other angle, where there is forgiveness available, it follows that certain actions—whether thoughts, words or deeds—can be dealt with only when one confesses and is forgiven. In short, the call to confession and the offer of forgiveness go hand in hand with the call to obedience. Cheap grace is grace without obedience, and the Elder knows no such grace. It is not the grace given to us in Jesus Christ.

Obedience: The Basis for Assurance (2:3) Even before we come to the question, What does God want of me? many of us may begin with another question, How can I be sure that I know God? Many faithful Christians struggle with this question. How do I know I'm a Christian? How can I be sure that I do indeed know God? How can I know that

---

The Greek phrase *peri holou tou kosmou* ("for the whole world") is an ellipsis; we should supply the word *sins,* as the NIV does in verse 2 *(for the sins of the whole world)* (Haas 1973:42; Houlden 1973:63; Marshall 1978:119 n. 31; Smalley 1984:40). The emphasis falls on the universal effectiveness of Christ's atoning work (Schnackenburg 1963:93), as the grammatical construction demonstrates *(ou monon . . . alla kai,* "not only . . . but also").

I'm not mistaken? The Elder assures his readers that they can have confidence before God. The confidence that he promises is not a subjective feeling or emotion. It is not necessarily equivalent to feeling good about ourselves. Confidence comes from knowing what God asks of us, and knowing that our aim is to live in conformity with God's standard. Now surely this sounds like a recipe to trouble souls, rather than for calming the troubled soul. And yet John speaks with encouragement and assurance as he promises *we know that we have come to know him.* Where does he derive such assurance?

The statement *we know that we have come to know him* is the first of many such statements offering assurance to the readers of the epistle (2:5; 3:19, 24; 5:2, 15; compare 2:18, 21, 29; 3:21; 4:13; 5:14, 18-20). Here the author is surely casting a glance at those who have left the church, for they undoubtedly claimed to know God. How does one decide between such personal and conflicting claims? Anyone can claim to know God. Is there a way to begin to assess that claim?

The Elder offers the "test" of obedience as the basis of having assurance of knowing God. Those who know God are obedient to the commands of God. And yet such a test scarcely seems calculated to offer the needed assurance to the readers! After all, John has just finished writing of the sinfulness of all people (1:8—2:2). Can one really depend, then, on one's obedience to God's commands to give assurance of right relationship to God? This idea is so central to 1 John that we must examine it more closely.

Obedience and Knowledge of God (2:4) It is important at the

Notes: 2:3 No meaningful distinction can be attributed to the author's use of two verbs for knowing, *ginōskō* and *oida* (Grayston 1984:63; Brown 1982:250). Although 1 John always uses *ginōskō* when speaking of knowing God or knowing Christ, the Gospel uses *oida* for the same purpose (8:19; compare 14:7). In other instances *oida* and *ginōskō* are virtually interchangeable (compare 1 Jn 3:14 with 3:19). On "knowing God," see Bultmann 1964:689-714; Dodd 1954:151-69; Marshall 1978:122.

The prepositional phrase *en toutō* (RSV, "This is how"; variously in NIV) appears twelve times in the epistle (2:3, 5; 3:10, 16, 19, 24; 4:2, 9-10, 13, 17; 5:2). One should be cautious of generalizations that the phrase more often or regularly points either forward or backward. Brown (1982:248-49) has a clear discussion and shows that when *en toutō* in a phrase is followed by a subordinate clause—as here, with the statement *if we obey his commands*— or a prepositional phrase, then the statement introduced by *en toutō* must refer forward in order not to leave the subordinate clause dangling, as the original NIV translation (*We can be sure we know him if we obey his commands)* assumes.

outset to put knowledge and obedience in the proper order. Obeying the commands of God is not a test we must pass in order to gain knowledge of God, a prerequisite of knowing God or a condition that must be fulfilled in order to come to know God. Rather, obedience is the manifestation or evidence of knowledge of God.

In light of what the Elder has written about human sinfulness and the need for confession, we can conclude that obeying God's commands does not require *perfect* obedience, if by perfect obedience we mean living without sinning. But obedience to God's commands should be more than an interesting addendum or occasional accompaniment to our lives. "Obeying God's commands" points to the shape of the Christian life as a whole, to the consistency of our discipleship, and not to individual acts taken in isolation. What is not in view is hollow adherence to a check list of rules or directions to be followed, as one follows a map to a destination or a recipe in a cookbook. If we try to map out obedience to God down to the last detail, then the life of faith loses its character as pilgrimage. Discipleship becomes an obstacle course to see whether we can negotiate each successive obstruction on our own. Obedience ceases to be response to a living God, and becomes instead a check list of rules. This is a dry and sterile view of Christian discipleship. I am reminded of the student who once asked, "Do you want us just to memorize this, or do we need to understand it?" Some Christians seem to live their lives with the grim intent to "just memorize it," enjoying none of the fullness and mystery that comes with wholehearted response to the God of our faith.

Him (auton) in 2:3 is ambiguous (as often in the epistle). Although the last-mentioned person is Jesus Christ, the pronoun probably refers to the Father here. What is at issue in the epistle is who truly claims to know God and how that knowledge is manifested. Specifically, in the context of this paragraph (2:3-6), the author addresses the question of what the life of one who knows the God who is light will look like. Thus the statement offers a positive criterion for knowing God, in contrast with the negative criterion of 1:6-10. The statements in 2:3 refer to 1:5 (Brown 1982:249; Smalley 1984:42). This also implies that in the phrases *his commands* (2:3-4) and *his word* (2:5) the pronoun refers to God.

2:4 The alternation between the participle *ho legōn (the man who says;* compare 2:6, 9), the if-clauses with a plural verb ("if we say"; 1:6, 8, 9, 10; 2:1) and the conditional relative clauses *(anyone,* 2:5) is stylistic. Brown (1982:253), however, suggests that the formulation "the one saying" (NIV, *the man who says)* may indicate that we have a direct quote from the secessionists, whereas "if we say" points to a paraphrase of claims of the secessionists.

Some readers may be frustrated to think that all we get by way of answer to the question, What does God want of us? is the response, Obedience to God's commands. But this is deliberate. We are not given directions, but direction. That direction can be summarized as "walking in the light," as striving to conform our character to that of God. What C. S. Lewis wrote in another context fits here: "We might think that God wanted simply obedience to a set of rules; whereas He really wants people of a particular sort" (1952:77). And the sort of people that God wants are those who hope to conform themselves to the very character of God.

Anyone who has had a hand in raising children knows about the process of shaping people of "a particular sort." When my daughter throws her food on the floor and I tell her not to do it, I am giving her a command that I would like to be obeyed. But in the end I do not want her to stop dropping her cereal on the floor just because I say so, but because she too recognizes the mess and waste it creates. Rules are given to guide behavior, but they are meant to be appropriated as internal guiding norms, not as external sanctions and prohibitions.

And yet we recognize that the words *obey his commands* direct the reader toward the concrete and practical. In the Elder's view, it is inevitable that what is interior must express itself in external and concrete action. "Knowledge of God" is not a sort of vague, unformed, abstract or indefinable private experience, although it may be extremely personal. "Knowledge of God" may express itself in various ways—through love and service to others, in prayer and worship of God, and so on. Here John is concerned to remind his readers that knowledge of God expresses itself in obedience, and obedience is always measured by concrete actions. After all, Jesus' obedience was made manifest in the ultimate sacrifice of his life on the cross.

Thus knowledge of and obedience to God are not entirely equivalent, nor are they unrelated to each other. We may best speak of "keeping God's commands" as *characteristic* of knowing God. " 'Keeping the commandments' (like fellowship with one another, 1:7) is not the condition, but rather the characteristic of the knowledge of God. There is no knowledge of God which as such would not also be 'keeping the commandments' " (Bultmann 1973:25). We might say that the question behind these verses is not, How do I get knowledge of God? but, What does knowledge of God look like? How does it express itself? So too the child who knows her parents well also knows their expectations well. And the child who loves and respects her parents, honors their expectations.

The idea that knowledge of God expresses itself in obedience has its roots in the Old Testament. The prophets especially spoke of knowing God, though more often they rebuked the people for not knowing God (Job 36:12; Jer 9:6; Is 1:3; 5:13; 1 Sam 2:12). The lack of knowledge of God does not imply intellectual inadequacy in comprehending God. Rather it points to a moral failure, to a lack of faithfulness and obedience. Those who know God live according to the way that God prescribes. "Knowing God" is understood in personal, intimate and relational terms.

To claim to love and know God without acknowledging God's claim upon us is simply hollow. Worse, it is a blatant contradiction in terms. Such a claim manifests a lack of relationship with God, a lack of being *in him* (v. 5). This phrase calls to mind a sphere in which we live our lives, a realm in which our decisions, choices, behavior and character are shaped. Those who are "in God" are those whose character and behavior are shaped by God's truth, righteousness and love (Kysar 1986:46). In fact, God's truth is viewed as something that is active, indwelling and powerful, something that shapes the person in whom it dwells. Obviously, then, those who have God's truth within them, and who know God, will manifest God's character.

In verse 6 the author speaks of this relationship with God with a new phrase, *live in him. Live* is the same word that older versions translated "abide"; other modern translations use "remain," or other variations. "Live" or "remain" strike those of us familiar with the old "abide" as colorless and flat. But the ordinary *live* serves well for "ordinary people." First, the term describes "the way in which a human life is determined by a fundamental relationship" (Kysar 1986:46; compare Marshall 1978:127). One lives either in the sphere of light or in the sphere of darkness. Our lives, our daily "walking," are shaped by the sphere in which we live. Second, in Johannine literature, *live* regularly connotes faithfulness, steadfastness, perseverance or continuing in allegiance to someone (Jn 8:31). It speaks to ordinary people of the consistency and faithfulness that is required of us. In short, the author's concept of "abiding" points to steadfast faithfulness. This is what God wants of us.

Obedience and Love for God (2:5) We come then to the assertion that *if anyone obeys his word, God's love is truly made complete in him.* Two important items should be noted. First, obedience and love of God are inseparably linked. Love of God, like knowledge of God, is expressed through "keeping God's word," through our allegiance to God. Second, note what the author does *not* say. He does not say that the more we obey, the more we show that we love God. In other words, the Elder is not criticizing Christians for failing to "do enough." Rather, his statement is directed at those who had left the church and who may have denied the need for obedience in the Christian life. John contends that it is simply impossible to claim to love or to know God without also living in obedience to God. In obedience to the commands, our love for God *is truly made complete,* that is, not made morally perfect or without flaw, but lived out as it should be.

Obedience and the Example of Jesus (2:6) The perfect expression of love for God is found in Jesus' own example. And so the Elder writes, *whoever claims to live in [God] must walk as Jesus did.* This statement seems to raise the stakes to an impossible level. Who can live like Jesus did? All of Jesus' life demonstrated obedience to God, and that obedience was manifested above all in his death on the cross (see Jn 5:19-20; 10:15, 17-18). Again, the point is not that we must manifest perfect obedience in all that we do. Rather we are to reflect on our lives, asking whether our thoughts, words and deeds show that our primary allegiance is to the God who is light.

The point of the admonitions to be obedient, to live righteously or to follow the example of Jesus is not to get us to start doing a number

---

2:5 The NIV *God's love* resolves the ambiguity of the phrase "love of God," which can be an objective genitive ("love *for* God"), a subjective genitive ("*God's* love") or a qualitative genitive ("God's *kind of* love"). Good sense can be made of any of these options, and it may be that an ultimate decision cannot or need not be made (see Marshall 1978:124-25). But in favor of the objective genitive ("love for God"; so also Stott 1988:96; Bruce 1970:51; Dodd 1946:31; Marshall 1978:125; Smalley 1984:49) note the parallel between verse 3, *We know that we have come to know him if we obey his commands,* and verse 5, *and whoever obeys [God's] word truly and fully loves God.* Knowledge of God and love of God are both manifested by obedience (Bruce 1970:51-52).

of things simply for the sake of doing them. Rather such admonitions remind us that we have already charted a course for ourselves. As we walk in that course we are reminded to ask ourselves, do these actions belong in the circle of light? The key here is reflection. We are not to be made anxious, but are rather prodded to reflect on what we say and do, how we think, pray, spend our time and money, raise our children, treat our coworkers, spouses and neighbors. Our aim is to live for one master, God alone, in and with all that we do. That is walking as Jesus walked.

So can we ever be *sure* that we know God? Some people have deep inner peace in their relationship with God. Others seem continually plagued by confusion and doubts. In seeking peace it is wise to keep the ends and means in proper order. Those who seek God are granted a sense of God's love and acceptance of them. This is the bedrock to which they return in times of crisis, discouragement and anxiety. Those who chase desperately for feelings of assurance usually do not find what they are looking for. If we focus on God and what God has done for us, we are oriented within the circle and guided by its fixed centerpoint. If we focus on ourselves or our own feelings, even with good intentions, we drift without direction or anchor.

The Fundamental Command: Love One Another (2:7-11) To answer the question, What does God want of us? on John's terms, we also have to answer the question, What do we owe each other? Although response to God is a personal matter, it is not merely a private or internal matter. Jesus made this explicit in talking about the obligation of love that we owe to each other in obedience to his command. Jesus does not require from us what he does not already manifest in his own person

---

The NIV takes the statement *This is how we know* in 2:5 to introduce what follows. It is possible that the phrase refers to what precedes. If so, it specifically has in view obedience to God's commands, not *God's love is truly made complete*, as the parallel with 2:3 suggests.

2:6 The NIV correctly assumes that a Greek demonstrative pronoun *ekeinos* ("that one") refers to Jesus and so translates it simply as "Jesus." In the epistles, although not in the Gospel, this is almost a formulaic way of referring to Jesus (3:3, 5, 7, 16; 4:17; see Marshall 1978:128). Here it surely refers to Jesus, since the command to "walk as he walked," although still undefined, makes better sense if it refers to the career of the earthly Jesus.

and life. In fact his sacrificial death both provides the example of love as well as creates the community in which we are to love one another.

The New Command (2:7-8) When John writes that one should *walk as Jesus did* (2:6), he goes on quickly to remind his readers that this is not a new commandment suddenly being imposed upon them. He is alluding to Jesus' command that the disciples are to "love each other as I have loved you" (Jn 15:12; compare 13:34). He also calls to mind the statement, "Greater love has no one than this, that he lay down his life for his friends" (Jn 15:13). It was Jesus who gave the command to love—but it was also Jesus who lived it out to the full in giving his life for "his own" (Jn 13:1). Years later when the author reminded his community of this command it was no longer new, but familiar and hence *old*, committed to them *since the beginning.* The command to love was part of that *message you have heard.*

What made the command new when Jesus gave it was not its content. The Old Testament contains the command to love one's neighbor (Lev 19:18), and Jesus quotes it in some of the Gospels (Mt 19:19; 22:39; Lk 10:27). Neither does Jesus have in mind a new kind of love or a new expression of love. The God whom Jesus knows and proclaims is a God of love (Jn 3:16).

But the command to love one another can be called new for two reasons: First, it points to a new example of love, that of Jesus' own life. We see his love most fully manifested in his death on the cross (compare Jn 13:1; 1 Jn 3:16; 4:9-10). Second, Jesus' death creates the new fellowship in which obedience to his command is possible. Jesus' death is the act by which all God's people can be gathered together (Jn 10:16; 11:51-52; 12:24). The command to love was given and modeled by Jesus, and now it is to be put into action by the believing community (2:8).

2:7 Here *ap' archēs, since the beginning,* and *the message you have heard* are mutually interpretative. The verse asserts that since the beginning of their life of faith (compare 2:24; 3:11; 2 Jn 6; Stott 1988:97; Grayston 1984:67; Houlden 1973:67) they have never heard another message *(logos,* as in 1:1, but not 1:5, where the idea is the same but the word is different, *angelia).*

The author alternates between the singular and plural of command. When using the singular he sometimes has in view Christian obedience to God, as a totality (2:6, *walk as Jesus did;* see 3:23; 4:21) and sometimes a specific command (2:8). The plural tends to emphasize the complete shape of love for God: it is manifested in obedience to God's commands (see also Brown 1982:251).

Through their love for one another they testify that the light brought into the world by Jesus' life continues to shine.

To use an analogy, the Christian community is the school in which we learn to love. Like great musicians who practice tedious drills for long hours, Christians practice their scales at home in order to sing in public. In the community love is commanded and modeled, and here is where it must be lived out and practiced. This does not mean that love is limited to the boundaries of the community. But if the community does not live by the model and teaching of its founder, Jesus, how can it expect others to do so or to hear its call to join with them?

The Incompatibility of Love and Hate (2:9-11) In fact, writes John, just as it is impossible to live simultaneously in two spheres—the sphere of light and the sphere of darkness—it is also impossible to live in the community and yet hate a fellow member of that community. Hate and love are incompatible; they repel each other like oil and water.

To be sure, hate is a strong term. It is difficult, if not impossible, to imagine that Christians who know the Johannine tradition of Jesus' command to love each other are openly advocating and practicing hatred for other Christians. That would be far too easy a target, and it is doubtful that the Elder would even need to refute such a position. Rather the hatred in this context refers to the actions of those who have left the church. John reminds his readers of the long-standing command to love each other, and asks whether those who have disrupted the fellowship are displaying obedience to that command. Hatred may not be a feeling, sentiment or emotion, as if those who are spoken of as hating their fellow Christians necessarily despise or detest them. But for John, their secession and disruption of the community is an action that speaks for itself.

2:7-8 The NIV's translation of verse 8, *Yet I am writing you a new command,* may be misleading if it is taken as referring to a new command in addition to the old command. The author views the same command, the command to walk as Jesus walked and, hence, to love as Jesus loved, in terms of its antiquity in the community and its new realization among that community (Brown 1982:266; Houlden 1973:67; Stott 1988:97-98; Marshall 1978:129).

2:8 The NIV apparently takes the relative clause "which is true in him and in you" to refer to the command itself: *its truth is seen in him and in you.* But command *(entolē)* is a feminine noun, and the clause "which is true in him and in you" begins with a neuter pronoun. It is better, then, to take the phrase as modifying the whole preceding idea.

Hatred is the opposite of the unity with each other that Jesus commanded. (For similar uses of the word *hate,* see Lk 14:26 and Rom 12:9.) Those who have turned away from other Christians show themselves to be dwelling in darkness. They can scarcely be said to know God, who is light. Thus, contrary to their claims that they know that they are on the path that leads to God, they *walk around in the darkness; [they do] not know where [they are] going, because the darkness has blinded [them].* In short, John is not so much concerned with how we "feel" about other Christians as he is with our intentions and actions to live in peace and harmony together. From such concrete actions, the sentiment of love may often spring. But unless our claims to love one another issue in concrete actions, then the claim to love each other—and to love God—rings false.

We must guard against a serious misinterpretation of verse 10 at this point. *Whoever loves his brother lives in the light* can be construed to mean that anyone who genuinely loves others is in fact walking in God's light. But that view misses two important items: First, it takes into account only one of the epistle's "tests of life." Confession of Christ provides another important boundary of the realm of light (2:22-23; 4:2; 5:5-8). Second, it fails to consider adequately the historical situation of the epistles. Against the backdrop of a specific problem and situation the epistle reminds its readers of the long-standing command to love each other. The statement *whoever loves* appears, on the surface, to mean "any one at all who loves." But the *whoever* should be taken in a more limited way. It refers to "the one of these two groups," and has in view specifically those loyal to the Elder, as over against the secessionists. In other words, John asks who truly manifests the love for their brothers and sisters that Jesus commanded, those who have left the fellowship or those who have remained?

Precisely their failure to interpret the command to love one's fellow Christian against the specific historical setting of these epistles has led some commentators to assert that the Johannine community knows

---

2:10 As the NIV notes, the prepositional phrase *in him* in the clause *there is nothing in him to make him stumble* can be translated "in it," referring to the light. But the translation *in him* is better, since it would be self-evident to say that there is nothing in the light that can make a person stumble. John notes that there is nothing in the believer to cause him

nothing of love for the world outside or for the unbeliever. But John does not say that we are not to love those outside the bounds of the Christian fellowship. Loving each other within the church and loving those outside the church are not mutually exclusive, even if the former is strongly emphasized in the Johannine epistles (Grayston 1984:65-66; compare Bultmann 1973:26 n. 9; Marshall 1978:132). We owe a special obligation of love to those within the Christian fellowship. This is in keeping with New Testament thought generally (1 Thess 3:12; 5:15; Gal 6:10). If it is stressed in 1 John, it is due to the situation of the times, as well as to the Christian community's peculiar obligation to manifest God's love to each other—and so extend the love of God to the world.

Encouragement to the Faithful (2:12-14) In some worship services, the congregation repeats the words of one of the creeds or confessions of the church on a regular basis. When the familiar words of the Apostles' Creed are spoken again, those who have gathered to worship are reminded of truths that the church has cherished throughout history. Some churches instruct young people and new converts through a series of classes, structured around a review of the "great truths" of Scripture and perhaps one of the classic catechisms of the church. And many churches use songs and choruses that invite their hearers to "tell me the old, old story" or "sing them over again to me." Reciting the foundational truths that Christians believe and hold dear need not be mindless repetition. Rather, when the church together recites, sings, studies or listens to the words of creed, confession, hymn or Scripture, read or recited repeatedly, it is also reminded of the faithfulness and constancy of God. We can depend on God to be the same *from the beginning.* This assurance of God's stability and faithfulness comes to light in 2:12-14.

Because the Elder is probably quoting familiar, creedlike statements in 2:12-14, many translations (including the NIV) set these lines off to look like a quotation. Just as we might quote a hymn, creed or verse of Scripture to remind ourselves what we believe and to what we are com-

---

(that is, himself, not another) to stumble. Compare Psalms 119:165, "Those who love your law have great peace; there is nothing in them that causes them to stumble"; Hosea 4:17, "By having become entangled with idols, Ephraim has placed a stumbling block for himself." *Stumble* does not refer to an occasional lapse, but to sinning by leaving the light.

mitted, so here the author quotes these lines to serve just such a purpose. John cites the lines at this point to take his readers back to the beginning of their faith, and to remind them of what they have always believed. He has talked about the message that they have had *from the beginning* (1:1; 2:7), and now he summarizes its content at greater length. His readers are to remember who they are and what they have been given.

Forgiveness in Christ (2:12) First, harking back to 1:6—2:2, John writes *because your sins have been forgiven on account of his name.* On the one hand, this statement serves as a reminder of the way in which they entered the community, namely, through confessing their sins and receiving God's forgiveness in Christ. On the other hand, the statement also speaks of the present reality of the need for forgiveness that is readily and continually available.

The phrase *on account of his name* refers to the "name" of Christ. In Semitic thought the "name" stands for the whole person. To "believe in the *name* of the Son of God" (1 Jn 5:13) means, quite simply, to believe in Jesus himself. Similarly, forgiveness *on account of his name* means forgiveness for his sake, or for the sake of what he has done. What is in view is primarily the *atoning sacrifice* of Jesus' death on the cross (2:2). Because of Jesus' sacrificial self-giving, God forgives sins through him. Those who have experienced this forgiveness are the children of God, the author's own *dear children,* the congregation of faithful believers.

Steadfast Knowledge of Christ (2:13a) While the epithet *dear children* refers here, as throughout the epistle, to all the church, the author next divides the congregation into *fathers* and *young men* (so NIV). It is not uncommon in the Bible for the whole people to be thought of as consisting of "young and old." Sometimes these categories refer to chronological youth and age, sometimes to spiritual youth and maturity.

Notes: 2:12 In verses 12-14 there are two sets of three parallel statements; however, the numbering of the verses does not coincide with the parallelism. Each statement opens with *I write to you.* In the first set of three, this verb is in the present tense; in the second set it is in the aorist. The NIV translates the verbs identically, thus assuming that the variation is merely stylistic. But the aorist may be slightly more emphatic. Whereas the present tense calls attention to what the author is writing at that moment, the shift to the aorist probably emphasizes that what the author is now writing is not at odds with what he has always written and proclaimed.

In addressing his readers as *children, fathers* and *young [people],* does the author have in mind one, two or three groups? The labels could refer to: (a) Christians viewed from

Jeremiah promises the people that when God inaugurates the new covenant, "they will all know [him], from the least of them to the greatest" (31:34). The prophet Joel, quoted by Luke in Acts, speaks of a time when "your old men will dream dreams, your young men will see visions" (Joel 2:28; compare Acts 2:17). Such language does not mean that only men are included, nor that those who are old experience one thing while the young experience another. Rather than pointing to divisions among the people, this language looks at the whole congregation, viewed from the least to the greatest, from new Christians to the mature, from young to old. What is true of one group is no less true of the other.

And yet it is not unfitting that John writes to those *fathers* that they have known the one who is *from the beginning.* By *fathers* he means those who have wisdom and maturity that comes with experience. *Fathers* need not connote men only, and we might render it as "elders," provided that we do not then think of church officers. In this verse it may be that Jesus Christ is the one who is *from the beginning.* Elsewhere in the epistle the Elder speaks of several things that have been "from the beginning," such as the message that has been delivered (2:24; 3:11; compare 1:1) and the command that has been passed on (2:7). What John means by such descriptions is not so much that these things have always existed—the command to love "as I have loved you," for example, was given in a particular historical place and time—but that as long as they have existed they have been the same. Both the foundational message that the Elder proclaims and the command to love have remained unchanged over the years. And Jesus Christ, the agent through whom God forgives sin, has not changed over the years either. If the "elders" came into the church through the forgiveness of Christ, they can be assured that he is the same, and that his forgiveness is constant—and

---

three aspects (hence, one group; so Dodd 1946:38-39); (b) to Christians *(dear children),* divided into old and young (hence, two groups); or (c) to three distinct groups *(children, fathers, young [people]).* Of these options the second is the most likely, since *dear children* regularly refers elsewhere in the epistle to Christians (2:1, 18, 28; 3:7, 18; 4:4; 5:21) and since Christian communities often distinguished among their adherents by their spiritual maturity, which was sometimes closely correlated with age as well (elders, youth; compare 1 Tim 5:1; 1 Pet 5:5; Tit 2:1-8).

The word translated *because (hoti)* can also be translated by "that" or rendered as quotation marks, introducing quotations. The author reminds his readers of certain truths that they know and at this point need to recall.

continually needed. Their knowledge of him does not need to undergo a radical transformation. Christ has been faithful, even as the "elders" have been faithful in their commitment to him.

Victory in Christ (2:13b) The Elder writes to those who are *young,* whether chronologically or spiritually, *because you have overcome the evil one.* Since youth and strength are often linked together, the epistle's words about overcoming are appropriately directed to those who are *young.* But here the imagery does not suggest physical strength so much as it does perseverance in the life of faith and commitment. These words are reminiscent of Isaiah 40:31, that "those who hope in the LORD will renew their strength. . . . They will run and not grow weary, they will walk and not be faint."

Like Paul, the author of 1 John views the struggle in which human beings are engaged as a struggle against "principalities and powers." For the *evil one* who is mentioned here is the devil (3:8, 12), the "one who is in the world" (4:4). John does not mean that God has abandoned this world to the power of evil, or that evil is stronger than God. As one hymn states it, "Although the wrong seems oft so strong, God is the ruler yet." So it is that those who *have been forgiven on account of his name* have *overcome the evil one.* Through the forgiveness that comes in Christ they have escaped from the power of the evil one, which manifests itself through slavery to sin and death (Jn 8:31-36). The Elder does not write that they *will* overcome or that they *can* overcome but that they *have* overcome. They have been transferred from death to life, from darkness to light. That they live in the sphere of light and life is their victory, their overcoming. Christians have overcome not by means of their own moral achievement, but through the victory over the power of evil won in Christ's death and resurrection (compare 1 Jn 3:8; 5:4-5, 18-19).

The Elder has a realistic view of what that victory implies. Already he has made it clear that it does not mean the Christian lives without sin in this life. Victory is not found in moral perfection, but in having the discernment to know the way to life and to walk in it. Now his readers

---

2:13 In both verses 13 and 14 the author writes that the "elders" have *known [the one] who is from the beginning.* While most commentators take this as a reference to Jesus Christ, a few think that it refers to God the Father, and some deem it deliberately ambivalent (Smalley 1984:74, 79; Grayston 1984:71; Marshall 1978:139-40). It may be that in the first

need to be admonished to take what was an initial choice and make it a continued commitment. Again, the metaphor of the path is appropriate, for victory is not a plateau that is attained but a path on which we have set out and on which we continue to walk.

Assurance of Knowledge of God (2:13c-14) Having outlined three central truths of the Christian life for his readers, John seems to start over by addressing, again, *children, fathers* (elders) and *young men* (people). He reiterates the same truths, but makes a few crucial changes. He reminds his *dear children* that what is ultimately at stake here is knowledge of God *(you have known the Father)*. Although the English translation obscures it, the author uses a different and more emphatic verb (the aorist) when he writes, *I write to you, dear children, because you have known the Father.* It is as if he says, "What I have written to you, I repeat: you have known the Father." What is striking is that in verse 12 he actually wrote to his *dear children* because *your sins have been forgiven.* That forgiveness was offered through the mediation of Christ. In this way the Elder links what he writes about knowledge of the *Father* to what he has written about forgiveness through *Christ:* the only way to knowledge of the Father is through "the name" of Jesus Christ.

Once again (v. 14) John writes to the elders that they *have known him who is from the beginning.* Whereas earlier this phrase characterized Jesus, here it seems to refer to the Father, mentioned in the previous verse. The Father is unchanging. If the "elders" were promised that they knew the Father as they made their initial confession of faith, they need not fear that their knowledge has proven defective in any way.

Finally, the young people are once again addressed. Again they are told, *you have overcome the evil one,* but two explanatory clauses are now added: *you are strong* and *the word of God lives in you.* Basically these two clauses express the same truth captured by the statement *you have overcome the evil one,* but with the added nuance of resisting false doctrine (Smalley 1984:79). For the Elder can speak not only of overcoming the evil one (2:13-14) and of overcoming the world (5:4), but

---

group of three statements (2:12-13a) John is thinking of Christ *who is from the beginning,* as the other material of these verses suggest, while in the second instance, it refers to the Father.

also of overcoming "them," the false prophets inspired by the spirit of antichrist (4:4). John promises his readers that in remaining faithful to the message they have always heard, they are remaining faithful to the very word of God. It lives in them. But because the dissidents have left the word of God, that word no longer abides in them.

In summary, then, this section demonstrates the same pastoral concern for building up the congregation that we have seen before. By reminding them of who they are and what they have been given, John assures his readers that they can be confident that they know God. Each statement of verse 14 describes the believer's standing in salvation: as children of God, they are strong, they have God's word abiding in them and have overcome the evil one. But these are not simply abstract truths or credal assertions. The author's point is twofold: First, we can have confidence with God because God is not capricious or fickle, arbitrarily tinkering with the truth or changing the grounds on which he is to be known. Second, this same, faithful God is not alien and distant, but knowable—knowable to *us,* knowable to *me*—in the love of Christ. What God revealed in Christ was not a new side of the divine character, but the confirmation of the love and forgiveness that have always characterized God's actions.

What the Elder writes is not new to his readers. But it serves a useful function to lay it all out again, to spell out exactly what constitutes the "way of life." By so doing, John prepares his readers for the warnings that follow (2:15-17). If they have chosen the way of life, the way of forgiveness and knowledge of God, they must continue in their commitment to it. For there is no other truth and no other way, except the love of the world—and that way is incompatible with the love of God.

Warnings Against Unfaithfulness (2:15-17) "In the world, but not of it"—this is a phrase commonly used to characterize the Christian's relationship to *the world.* And yet many and varied are the opinions

---

Notes: 2:15 *Love of the Father* should be taken as an objective genitive, "love *for* the Father." This provides a better parallel with the command *do not love the world* (implied: but love God). It also provides a logical conclusion to the "if" clause: if anyone loves the world, then they do not love God (for the two are mutually exclusive). Moreover, this translation anticipates the reason given in verse 17 that *the [one] who does the will of God*

about what constitutes "worldliness." Many religious groups and denominations forbid, either explicitly or implicitly, certain behaviors. In some circles smoking is forbidden; some groups look down on drinking alcoholic beverages, dancing, rock music or attending movies. And yet in other groups, cultures or countries, other strictures may be in place, while those just listed are not. A Christian from an Eastern European country once told me that in his circles attending public sporting events was frowned upon. Some stricter groups have avoided the use of modern machinery and automobiles.

The common thread in avoiding "worldliness" is the desire to conform one's life to the will of God and not to the dictates of the world. Obviously this is a laudable goal. And although the present passage does not give us rules and regulations, it does make plain the incompatibility of love for the world and love for God. But the conception of worldliness in this epistle goes far deeper than the idea of outlawing some behaviors that non-Christians tolerate. We are called to an active devotion to God that shapes all that we are and do. Barclay captures the essence of the passage when he entitles it "Rivals for the Human Heart" (1976:55). The world is not simply a passive entity, but a rival for the allegiance of every person.

Do Not Love the World (2:15) But what exactly is the *world* that the Christian disciple is commanded not to love? John 3:16 asserts that God "loved the world." Are God's children to do less? Too often Christians live as though they were of the world, but not in it. They have adopted the good things of culture and society, but refuse to involve themselves to create positive change. They take credit for the good, but shift the blame for the bad. John does not mean that Christians are to shun involvement in secular or political affairs, or that they are not to care about and for that which we call "the world." What, then, does the command *do not love the world* really mean?

We are helped by noting that in Johannine thought *world (kosmos)*

---

lives forever. Those who do God's will are those who love God. (See Brown 1982:306; Marshall 1978:143-44; Schnackenburg 1963:127.) Others (Haas 1972:58; Houlden 1973:73; Smalley 1984:83) translate the genitive as "the love which belongs to the Father." If this is the case, John means that love for the world is proof that God's love does not dwell in that person.

is used in a variety of ways. First, *world* can refer, positively, to that which God created (Jn 1:9-10) or a realm where one exists (8:23; 9:5; 10:36; 11:27). Second, it also may refer to the people who inhabit the world (Jn 1:10; 3:16-17; 4:42; 6:51; 7:4; 8:12, 26; 9:5; 12:19, 47). God's love is directed toward them, but their response to that love is mixed (3:17-21; 9:39). Third, *world* is used more negatively and characteristically to designate those who reject or ignore God (or Jesus), those who live without recognizing the claims of God upon them. We find this negative usage of *world* often (Jn 1:10; 3:17; 8:23; 9:39; 12:31; 14:17, 19, 22; 15:18-19). That this world is in the power of the evil one (12:31; 14:30; 16:11) and hence opposed to God is particularly emphasized in 1 John (4:4; 5:19). Nevertheless, God still loves the world and sent the Son to destroy the works of the devil (3:8, 16). The following diagram illustrates the negative usage of *world* in this passage:

(A) The world   (B) with its values   (C) is passing away.

(a) The one who obeys   (b) the will of God   (c) remains forever.

Those who are "the world" stand over against those who obey. What makes the world "worldly" is its persistent rejection of the claims of God in favor of its own values and desires. In this passage, *world* and *anything in this world* designate a complex web of values, decisions and directions in life chosen without consideration for knowing and doing the will of God. When the Elder writes *do not love the world* he in essence calls people to make a choice for God's way of doing things and not for the world's ways.

But how does this square with the statement of John 3:16 that God loved the world? In that well-known verse God's love is demonstrated by the sending of the Son, an act intended to "save the world." God saves people who are bound by the world and its values by freeing them from their captivity. Quite simply, loving the world does not mean accepting it as it is, but remaking it into what it was created by God to be: people living in the realm of life and light.

The command *do not love the world* demands that we reject those ways of life which do not lead us to God or to the practice of truth, justice, righteousness and love. While this sounds easy enough in theory, it is not easy in practice. For it entails the recognition and condemnation of sin and unrighteousness. Here we can too easily fall prey to arrogant judgmentalism on the one hand or, on the other hand, to the subtle tug to let sinful behaviors pass unnoticed or unnamed in our efforts to love and accept people as they are. And yet acceptance and love of others never means that we must—or may—approve of a way of life that is inimical to God's way of light. Certainly Jesus knew his ministry to be one that exposed sin (Jn 16:8-10). Yet a ministry of exposing the unrighteousness of the world's ways does not stand in contradiction to a ministry of love. For precisely by exposing sin, lies and hatred, we can become channels of God's truth, light and love, so that we enable others to live in that truth as well. But let us remember the epistle's admonitions to confess our own sins, and so let judgment begin at home.

The Essence of Worldliness (2:16-17) "Worldliness" cannot then be neatly packaged into certain behaviors that the devout believer avoids. And yet John continues with two verses that sound rather like a dire warning about the nature of worldliness. Indeed, the NIV's vivid translation—that the sinner exhibits cravings, lust and pride—leaves little doubt that these impulses are to be resisted. But what are these impulses that characterize the "world" but should not characterize those who are "in but not of" the world?

First comes the phrase *the cravings of sinful man.* The word *cravings* *(epithymia)* is the same word translated as *lust* in the next phrase. Craving may be neutral in its connotations, meaning simply longing or desire, and often in the New Testament it has this sense. The NIV translates the Greek "flesh" *(sarkos)* as *sinful man.* But flesh can be positive in the Johannine literature. Both the Gospel (1:14; 6:51-55; compare 17:2) and epistle (1 Jn 4:2) unashamedly state that Jesus Christ has come in the flesh. "Flesh" means the human realm, which, in itself, is not evil or negative. But insofar as it stands apart from God, it must be reborn through the power of the spirit (Jn 6:63), or it remains lifeless and dead (Jn 3:6). Just as a body without breath cannot live, so flesh without Spirit cannot live eternally.

Hence *the cravings of sinful man* are "desires that come from the flesh," or "human striving." This means desire that is shaped by the world unaware of and untouched by God, all those desires and plans that are shaped entirely by our impulses and not by the Spirit of God. The criticism of the "desire of the flesh" rests not on the fact that such desires come from sin—for "flesh" need not have that meaning—but on the fact that they do not come from the Spirit. Had John given some examples relevant to today, he surely would have included this culture's pervasive materialism, workaholic ethic, sexual laxity and driving desires for success and prosperity. Any attitude or action that makes the individual—and not God—the center and measure of the universe smacks of worldliness. "Worldliness" is serving many gods, be they personal whims, ambitions or strivings.

Just as flesh is the source of the *craving* in the previous phrase, so here human *eyes* are the source of the lust in the next phrase. We might translate *lust of his eyes* as "desire that comes from what the eyes see." These desires do not come from the insight that God gives, but are shaped by the world in its ignorance of or opposition to God. They may include greed, materialism and envy, for later the Elder warns those who do not aid their brothers and sisters in need (3:16). Those held by the grip of the world lust for what they see, and not for what the Spirit gives them eyes to see as good.

The third phrase in this trio is *boasting of what he has and does.* The pride spoken of is self-reliance, self-sufficiency. Either people trust in themselves, or they derive their values, assurance and life from God. It is exactly this attitude of self-sufficiency, seeing things in our own light and not by the light of God, that the Elder terms "worldliness."

Those who live this way experience a futile existence, dedicated to things that are short-lived and offer little lasting satisfaction, for *the world and its desires pass away.* John means that God's light, already shining (2:8), has overcome the power that animates the world of darkness (2:12-14). Those who put their trust in earthly possessions commit their

---

2:16 Examples of a neutral use of *desire* include Philippians 1:23, "I desire to . . . be with Christ," Luke 22:15 and 1 Thessalonians 2:17.

Other neutral uses of "flesh" in the New Testament include Matthew 16:17, Galatians 1:16 and John 17:2. In the first two examples the phrase "flesh and blood" (NIV *man*) denotes what is human, as opposed to what is from God, without necessarily viewing it in a negative light. The phrase "desire of the flesh" (NIV "sinful nature") appears in Pauline writings in Galatians 5:16-17 (see 5:24), where "flesh" designates that which is sinful. Compare 1 Peter 4:2-3 and 2 Peter 2:10. Desire may include, but is not limited to, sexual desire or lust.

energies and selves to a sphere whose end has already been assured. They strive to live by a power that has been drained of its source of energy and is now running on empty.

This passage, then, is a manifestation of the Johannine dualism. One loves either God or the world. This theme echoes throughout Scripture. The first commandment is "You shall have no other gods before me." Joshua commanded the children of Israel to "choose for yourselves this day whom you will serve. . . . As for me and my household, we will serve the LORD" (24:15). Jesus warned, "No one can serve two masters. Either he will hate the one and love the other, or he will be devoted to the one and despise the other. You cannot serve both God and Money" (Mt 6:24). And now the author of 1 John, like his master Jesus, reminds people that there can be only one allegiance, one loyalty, which shapes all that we are and do. There is no way to play both ends against the middle. The commands of this passage are to be heard both as an *invitation* to serve God and, for those who have heard and responded to such an invitation, as an *exhortation* to continue to make that response daily.

Warnings Against Antichrists (2:18-27) Now and again a story appears in the news about the passing of counterfeit money. Often counterfeit bills are discovered when an unsuspecting consumer tries to use one, not realizing that the money is in fact worthless. Usually the differences between real and counterfeit currency are so subtle that none but experts can tell them apart. And yet one isn't even worth the paper it's printed on, while the other can be redeemed for its face value—whether $10 or $100 or $1,000.

The warnings against antichrists in 2:18-27 are warnings against counterfeit teachers and the beliefs they are passing out among the unsuspecting. These teachers and their followers may have held beliefs that

---

For *alazoneia* see James 4:16, Romans 1:30 and 2 Timothy 3:2. The word connotes pride, arrogance and boastfulness. It also may mean ostentatious displays of power, success or wisdom, and the phrase *alazoneia tou biou* can be translated "overconfidence stemming from the security of one's life" (see Brown 1982:311-12).

2:17 Smalley (1984:87) suggests that the statement *the world and its desires pass away* may refer to the created world (Marshall 1978:146-47; but see Schnackenburg 1963:131-32). The contrast is not between heavenly and earthly realms, but between two kinds of people, those who do the will of God, and those who do not (Stott 1988:106).

seemed to differ only minimally and subtly from those of the Elder and his congregations. But when examined with care against the standard of measure, they are shown to be worthless, cheap imitations of the one real thing of great value: a true and abiding faith.

By labeling these false teachers as *antichrists* the Elder makes it plain how seriously he regards their offense. If in 2:15-17, John spoke of opposition between God and the world, he now speaks of one way in which that opposition is manifested in a visible and concrete form, namely, in the defection from the fellowship of a number of professed believers.

The Appearance of Antichrists (2:18-19) The Elder begins with the bold assertion that *this is the last hour.* In the New Testament only here do we find this formulation *(eschatē hōra).* Some similar phrases, however, are found elsewhere in the New Testament.

"The last days" refer to the days in which God's plan of salvation for the world is brought to fruition (Acts 2:17; Joel 2:28; Mic 4:1). From this perspective it can be said that "the end" has come (compare 1 Cor 10:11). But the "end" is not a fleeting moment. It is rather a period that marks a new stage in God's dealings with the world.

Other passages (2 Tim 3:1; Jas 5:3; 2 Pet 3:3) take "the last days" as the final days of the interim period between Christ's coming and his return. These last days are distinguished from the day of the Lord (Acts 2:17, 20), the day of judgment (2 Pet 3:3, 7) or the Second Coming and final judgment (2 Tim 3:1; 4:1, 8).

The Gospel of John speaks of "the last day" (Jn 6:39-40, 44, 54; 11:24; 12:28), which refers to a future day of resurrection and the final judgment. Yet the Gospel of John also emphasizes that Jesus' mission has the effect of passing judgment in the present. Those who believe already have life, while those who do not already are judged. The "last day" seals the present verdict (3:17-21; 5:25-27).

John also speaks of the hour of Jesus' death and glorification on the cross as the "hour" (see Jn 2:4; 7:30; 8:20), a decisive time and turn of events in the unfolding drama of salvation.

Notes: 2:18 The absence of the definite article before *last hour* does not make it indef-

Against the background of these various last hours and days, where do we fit the statement that *this is the last hour?* Many take it to mean that the Elder believed that his community was at the end of those "last days," at the final hour before the "last day" (Dodd 1946:51; Bruce 1970:64; Houlden 1973:77; Brown 1982:321). But two facts must be kept in mind here: First, in Johannine vocabulary, "hour" can refer to a decisive event or occurrence rather than to a unit of chronological time. It is instructive to note that the command that is linked with the statement *this is the last hour* is the command to abide, or to remain steadfast and faithful (compare vv. 19, 24, 27). This suggests that *hour* is a decisive event, in light of which steadfastness is particularly necessary; chronological consider- ations may not be primary. But something has happened that demands all the vigilance and faithfulness of believers.

Second, in Johannine eschatology, the judgment and blessings expect- ed in the last days are already taking place through Jesus. What had been expected in the future, such as final judgment, the separation of the righteous and wicked, and the granting of eternal life to the righteous, was already effected through the ministry and death of Christ. The Elder sees the realities of separation and judgment being worked out in his own situation. They do not eliminate the last judgment. Rather, judgment is already being passed in the present.

Specifically, of course, the author has in mind the secession of certain members from the church, a separation that shows that those who have left the fellowship have passed judgment upon themselves (compare Jn 3:17-21). The New Testament regularly speaks of signs that will presage the end (such as Mk 13:4-5; 2 Thess 2:1-12; 2 Tim 3:1-5). Among these telling events are false teaching, behavior unworthy of a believer and divisions in the church and among friends and family. Exactly these things characterize the situation behind this epistle and are part of the landscape that the Elder sees. These signs signal that the decisive event by which God passes judgment and grants salvation has indeed occurred.

It is then the *last hour,* and the judgment of God, expected in Jewish eschatology at the end times, is indeed manifesting itself. Judgment

---

inite, "it is a last hour" (Westcott 1966:69; Morris 1970:1266; compare Marshall 1978:148 n. 1; Smalley 1984:97).

entails separation of evil from good, right from wrong, truth from error. Such separation is taking place already in the historical situation of the Johannine church. *They went out from us,* the writer asserts (2:19). Here is the first explicit mention of the secessionists who departed from the fellowship of the church. Until this point, the readers have inferred their existence from various statements, and John's polemic against them has been indirect only. Now, however, it is clear that there are some who have left the church. When this epistle was written, the initial rupture in the community lay in the past, but it seems that the threat of further defection is still real. Perhaps some who are still faithful to the Elder are being pressured to abandon him and join the secessionists (see v. 26). But, on the whole, John is looking back and interpreting the split as evidence of the nearness of the last hour, and of the outworking of the judgment expected at that time.

In light of the reality of judgment and of the present possibility of receiving the great blessings of God promised to believers, the call to remain steadfast is always urgent. For John, the question of the time of the last judgment is of secondary importance. For regardless of when the final judgment is to come, God's judgment is now being put into effect when people acknowledge or deny Jesus as Messiah and Son of God. How much more important to recognize God's work in Christ as bringing eternal life and judgment *now* than to be able to decode timetables about when the last judgment will break! To date no apocalyptic speculation has proved itself correct. But the epistle's message that the great judgment, the "sifting" of the church (Barclay), occurs as one responds to Jesus, has eternal relevance. There is the heart of John's warning, *this is the last hour.*

2:19 Marshall (1978:151 n. 10) dismisses Bultmann's claims that the secessionists continued to regard themselves as "legitimate members" of the Johannine community; but compare Smalley 1984:102-3. The defectors may well have considered themselves as the legitimate interpreters and heirs of the tradition of the community.

The repetition of *ex hēmōn* (four times) is emphatic (Smalley 1984:102). Probably there is also a play on the meaning of the phrase, for it can suggest either (a) membership in a group ("they quit our fellowship") or (b) origin or location ("they went out *from us*") (Haas 1972:63). The author means that their physical departure manifested their lack of real belonging to the fellowship (so Smalley 1984:101: "they withdrew from us, but they did not belong to us").

There are several difficulties in the Greek translated by the statement *their going showed that none of them belonged to us (hina phanerōthōsin hoti ouk eisin pantes ex hēmōn).* (1) The NIV supplies *their going* for the *hina* clause; one could supply *touto egeneto* ("this

John refers to these secessionists as *antichrists*. This term is found in the New Testament only in the Johannine epistles (1 Jn 2:18, 22; 4:3; 2 Jn 7). It may well have been coined by the Johannine community or perhaps by the Elder himself. The antichrist opposes Christ, but not so much by open aggression and hostility as with deceit and falsehood. The antichrist usurps the rightful role of the Messiah, the Christ, and deceives his followers (Houlden 1973:77; Marshall 1978:150; Smalley 1984:99; Stott 1988:109). The antichrist is, in short, a counterfeit Christ. Apparently the community is familiar with the expectation that such a figure will appear and that this appearance will mark the "last days." What is distinctive here is that the term is used in the plural, and so in a way this differs from the expectation of the readers. Evidently not merely one figure embodying great evil, but *many* individuals who manifest that ultimate error have appeared on the scene (see Mk 13:22; Mt 24:3, 5, 11; compare Rev 16:13; 19:20; 20:10; 2 Thess 2:1-12).

The *antichrists* of 1 John are those who deceive others through false teaching about the person of Christ and the nature of the Christian life (2:22-23; 4:2). There are genuine theological disagreements between these false teachers and the author, and he will soon deal with the issues. But it is not only disagreement about formulations of doctrine that stimulates John to write. It is impossible not to sense his distress and anger over the actual departure of these people as well. The breaking of fellowship is in itself judged quite severely, and seems to have taken a greater toll on the church than have the actual reasons for it (Barker 1981:324). This sin is as bad as, if not worse than, the actual doctrinal error, because in leaving the fellowship these secessionists have disre-

---

happened") or *exēlthan* ("they went out"), which leaves the statement more ambiguous. (2) For ease of translation, the NIV uses a past tense *(showed)* for the subjunctive verb. But the Greek construction may well indicate that the departure occurred *in order to* reveal the true character of the dissidents. Dodd (1946:52), Houlden (1973:78) and Smalley (1984:104) suggest that the purpose clause points ultimately to God's providence in this matter (compare Jn 6:44-45; 17:12); the defection already indicated God's judgment. (3) The subject of the *hoti* clause is ambiguous. It may refer to the dissidents, in which case it means "all are not of us" (RSV) or *none of them belongs to us* (NIV). It may refer to the congregation, in which case it means "not all [church] members belong to us" (NEB). Since verse 18 introduces the problem of *antichrists* who have not *remained with us* (v. 19), it is more likely that the reference is to those who have obviously left the fellowship, not to some who may still be lurking within it.

garded the cardinal and foundational command of Jesus to "love each other." In fact, the author's ultimate judgment on the heretics is due as much to their secession as to their doctrinal aberrations (Houlden 1973:78). We see here the community's commitment to unity, as they believed Jesus taught, commanded and died for (Jn 10:16; 11:52; 17:21). We also sense their horror of professed disciples who fall away and deny the Lord, such as Judas (Jn 6:66-71; 13:18-30) and, very nearly, Peter (Jn 13:36-38).

It is probably difficult for Christians today who are accustomed to a church with a multitude of denominations to take seriously the problem of schism or defection. But too often new congregations and denominations are formed as the result of disagreements or disputes, with at least one faction convinced that it alone understands and correctly interprets the will of God in matters of doctrine and polity. And the urge to reform the church thus becomes the practice of splitting the church. Although the sixteenth-century Reformers may be invoked as exemplars of the crusade for truth and the purity of the church, seldom is it remembered that they strove also to preserve the unity of the church by working toward agreements with each other and with the Roman Catholic church. Although their efforts often failed, like John they cherished the unity of the church and deplored its divisions.

In this light, we do well to remember the words of the Gospel of John, where Jesus said, "I have other sheep that are not of this flock [sheep pen]. I must bring them also. They too will listen to my voice, and there shall be one flock and one shepherd" (10:16). Because the work of Jesus unites us, we must take care lest our own work divides us from others who name the name of Christ. At the least, our efforts to live in fellowship and work side by side with other Christians will prevent us from

---

2:20 *Anointing* may refer either to the *substance* (such as oil) with which one is anointed (Bultmann 1973:37; Marshall 1978:153, Smalley 1984:105) or to the *act* of anointing (Brown 1982:342-43). If it refers to the act of being anointed, it may be taken *literally*, with reference to a ritual action of anointing, or *figuratively*, in that it compares an act such as baptism to anointing, or else refers more generally to a divine gift of some sort. Despite the denials of Brown (1982:341), it is likely that the secessionists would have claimed an *anointing* as well. This is why the claim must be tested by external evidence (such as action and belief).

That *the Holy One* refers to God is argued by Dodd (1946:53), Houlden (1973:79) and Stott (1988:111); that it refers to Jesus is accepted by Schnackenburg (1963:153), Haas (1972:64), Bultmann (1973:37), Marshall (1978:155), Barker (1981:325), Brown (1982:348)

thinking that we alone comprise the one true flock for which the Good Shepherd laid down his life.

The Anointing of "the Holy One" (2:20-21) Having made it clear to his readers that those who left the community have revealed that they never really belonged there, the Elder now turns to assure his readers of their firm standing in God's care and in the Christian community. However, the statement with which he offers such assurance remains ambiguous to us. *You have an anointing from the Holy One, and all of you know the truth* raises several questions for the modern reader. What is the nature of this anointing? Who is the Holy One? And what is the truth that is known by all? What is clear is that John appeals to a teaching or power that comes from beyond the believer. By this anointing believers may discern the truth.

But what does the Elder have in mind when he speaks of such an anointing? In light of the parallels to statements about the Paraclete, the Holy Spirit, in the Gospel of John, it may be that the anointing spoken of here is the gift of the Holy Spirit. The Spirit of truth guides believers into the knowledge of the truth and teaches them "all things" (Jn 14:17, 26; 15:26; 16:13). The Spirit remains or abides *(menein)* in believers. The Spirit testifies about Jesus (15:26; 16:13-15), even as believers now also do. In short, the anointing of which believers may be confident is the presence and guidance of the Spirit of Truth.

The identification of the anointing as the Spirit who enables the discernment of truth does not tell us *how* the Spirit enables such discernment. Is the Elder speaking of an internal, private, subjective experience of the Spirit's leading? In view of his regular appeals to what has been taught and heard and believed "from the beginning," sudden appeal to an inner guiding light seems unlikely. It would, after all, open the doors

and Smalley (1984:108); that it means the Spirit is asserted by Grayston (1984:87), Kysar (1986:61), Morris (1970:1266) and Smith (1991:72). Grayston (1984:87) perceptively notes that because the secessionists deny that Jesus is the *Christ* (v. 22), it is unlikely that Jesus can also be the *Holy One* who grants the anointing. The ultimate appeal must be to the one who inspires confession of Jesus as the Christ, and this happens by the Spirit of God (compare 4:1-6).

There is a textual variant at the end of verse 20. Some manuscripts read "you know all things" *(oidate panta)* while others read "you all know" *(pantes oidate)*, leaving the object to be supplied (NIV *the truth*, from v. 21). *Pantes* has better textual support. The stress falls on what all, not a few, know.

for the Elder's opponents to enter the same claim. More likely, it is the teaching itself, the content or message, and its continuity with the word of earliest times that John takes as evidence of the Spirit's continued abiding with and anointing of the community. The guiding work of the Spirit cannot be separated from the content and shape of the message itself. When claims to have the Spirit's inspiration result in teachings or practices that either contradict or seem far more informed on certain points than Scripture itself, it is a clear sign that it is not the inspiration of God's Spirit that is at work.

There is some ambiguity about the identity of *the Holy One,* for it is unclear whether the reference is to the Father, Son or Spirit. In the Gospel of John, Peter confesses that Jesus is the "Holy One of God," and Jesus is the one who sends the Paraclete from the Father (15:26). And yet the Gospel also states that God sends the Spirit (14:16, 26), and in 1 John this is more clearly the case (3:24; 4:1, 13; compare 5:8-9). Finally, the Gospel does speak of the Spirit as "the Holy Spirit" (14:26). In short, one could argue that *the Holy One* refers to Father, Son or Spirit and find support for that decision in the Johannine literature.

We get some help by noticing the play on words in the present passage: the words *antichrist, anointing* and *Christ* all have the same root *(christos, chrisma).* A true anointing *(chrisma)* enables a true confession of Christ *(Christos);* but those who are not anointed by the Spirit of God are, in fact, antichrists *(antichristoi).* "Christians"—"anointed ones"—are to test the "spirits," that they may know which Spirit is "from God" (4:2-3). God the Father gives the Spirit who inspires true understanding and confession of Jesus the Son. Thus God is the final court of appeal. It would be crucial for the Johannine Christians to be able to claim the ultimate source of the Spirit with which they had been anointed and which continues to guard the truth of their confession. Their Spirit does not come from the evil one and is not a source of error; the Spirit they know comes from God and guards the truth. It is also worth noting in

---

2:21 *Hoti* here should perhaps be "that" (not *because* as in the NIV) in each instance. The Elder is not citing reasons why he is writing, but reminding his readers that they do indeed know the truth and that they therefore ought to recognize that no lie is from the truth (so also Brown 1982:350; Bultmann 1973:38; Culpepper 1985:48; Marshall 1978:156 n. 30; Schnackenburg 1963:154 n. 6; Smalley 1984:110).

passing the trinitarian tendencies of John's statements about the way in which the work of God, the Son and the Spirit are in reality one inseparable work of salvation.

The *anointing*, the guiding of the Spirit, insures that *all of you know the truth.* That anointing is not limited to a few or to the elite: it belongs to all. By *all*, of course, the author means all within the sphere of his church and readership. What they know the elder calls *the truth.* He is not saying that all believers know all the truth there is to know, but rather that his community is acquainted with the truth that their opponents deny. They know the truth about the disputed issues, and they do not need further teaching or some additional insight into the person of Jesus Christ, such as the false teachers may have claimed to possess and to offer (compare 2:27). What the false teachers espouse is in reality a great lie.

The Great Lie (2:22-23) The truth that the community confesses and that the liar, the antichrist, denies, is that *Jesus is the Christ.* Stated in these terms, it might appear that the Elder's rebukes are directed against Jewish opponents who did not see in Jesus the hoped-for Messiah. Yet that is probably too simple. To begin with, it does not adequately explain how such people could ever have been part of a Christian fellowship at all. For it seems that those who had left the church had appeared at one point to be true believers. But it is very difficult to decide exactly what the dissidents were advocating and what the author feels compelled to defend against them. Broadly speaking, the *liar* is anyone who claims knowledge of God apart from the revelation in Jesus Christ (Culpepper 1985:58). More specifically, the liars are the defectors from the community. But what exactly are they denying?

Here we must take into account other statements from the epistle. The affirmation that "Jesus Christ has come in the flesh" (4:2; 2 Jn 7), and that he is the one who came by water and blood (5:6) suggest that the mere identification of Jesus as the "Messiah," while important, is not the

---

2:22 The NIV's translation *It is the man who denies . . .* renders a Greek participle that may be translated "It is the one who denies. . . ," referring to *the evil one,* the chief liar (3:8-15; see Jn 8:44: the devil is a liar and the "father of lies"); compare Kysar (1986:62).

On the confession that Jesus is the Messiah, note John 9:22, where people are apparently expelled from the synagogue on the basis of this confession; see also 16:2.

ultimate issue. Moreover, we can view these statements almost as slogans, as pithy summaries of emphases found elsewhere in the Gospel and epistles. As a human being who "lived among us" (Jn 1:14; 1 Jn 1:2) and who died to atone for sins (1 Jn 1:7; 2:1-2), Jesus mediates salvation and eternal life, and is therefore the way to knowledge of and fellowship with God (Jn 14:6; 17:3; 1 Jn 1:7).

All these truths have at their heart the affirmation that Jesus makes God known and so mediates the way to knowing God. The use of the title "Christ" or "Messiah" fits into this category of "mediation" as well. On the one hand, the Messiah was, by definition, to be God's chosen and anointed delegate in ruling the kingdom. To follow the Messiah was to obey God's chosen one, and so to obey God. Thus the term "Christ" or "Messiah," when applied to Jesus, does say something about his identity; and what it says is that he is God's accredited agent in establishing the reign or kingdom of God (Houlden 1973:80). The dissidents may not have disagreed with this statement; they may not even have denied that Jesus is the Messiah. But the Elder asserts that in their actions they effectively do deny his function in mediating knowledge of God and eternal life (2:25). That is what their secession from the community reveals.

"Messiah" is thus the author's shorthand summary for his understanding of Jesus. It entails far more than the confession of Jesus as an expected figure of Jewish eschatology. The "more" that Messiah connotes for John is made clear in the bold assertion that to deny the Son is in fact to deny the Father (2:23). We move from language of God and Messiah to the familial terminology of Father and Son, which stresses the intimate relationship that exists between them. Typical of 1 John, this assertion is made negatively, *denies the Son,* with an eye toward those who went out, and positively, *acknowledges the Son,* with an eye toward the faithful community. Those in the faithful community not only know God, they *[have] the Father;* that is, they have God as Father. If Jesus is the unique Son, those who acknowledge that Son are children of God (3:1-2; Kysar 1986:63).

In this context, "denying" and "acknowledging" have two aspects: a cognitive dimension, the dimension of true understanding, as well as the matter of discipleship or following Jesus. For to deny Jesus is to deny the true and accepted understanding of him, such as has been *heard from the beginning* (v. 24). But, second, denial of Jesus is also a "failure of allegiance" to him (Houlden 1973:80). Those who left the fellowship of believers have in fact faiĺed in their allegiance to Jesus himself.

The positive "acknowledging Jesus" entails holding a true understanding of him and his atoning and intercessory work (1:7-10; 2:1-2). John lays out how we must understand Jesus and what he has done. Having understood the how of Jesus' mediating work, we also acknowledge Jesus in commitment and loyalty to him. Thus to acknowledge Jesus is to accept his command to love (2:7-11) and to walk in his example of single-minded obedience to God (2:6, 15-17). That is, "acknowledging Jesus" means recognizing both *that* he mediates salvation and *how* he mediates salvation. These truths are so integrally interrelated that the author speaks of them simply as *the truth* (2:21). And it is especially at the point of the way in which Jesus mediates salvation, *how* salvation comes to us, that John and the schismatics disagree, as the Elder's earlier words about the necessity of accepting the atoning work of Jesus (1:7—2:2) have already made clear.

Here then is a reminder to the church that the message it dare not sacrifice is the "stumbling block of the cross," to borrow a phrase from Paul. Any version of the Christian message that abandons the twin truths of human sin and divine salvation through the cross of Jesus would fall outside of John's rubric of *the truth*. The very real danger facing John's church and the church today is to water down and ignore the realities of human sinfulness and God's demand. And this happens in many ways. It happens when the gospel is turned into a panacea for the problems, big and small, that we all face, and the sum and substance of the gospel becomes a promise for a better life defined on our terms. It happens when we preach only what God generously gives to us and not what God also expects of us. It can happen when human beings label as acceptable what the Scriptures label as intolerable: injustice, unkindness, intolerance, immorality, hatred, greed, selfishness and so on. And it happens when alternative ways to knowing God—whether in other religions or movements, such as the New Age movement—are condoned as acceptable ways of salvation.

Exhortations to Faithfulness (2:24-27) The author reminds his readers that what he is now telling them is in fact what the church has *heard from the beginning.* He warns them against those who are trying to lead them astray from that well-founded teaching which *remains in you.* Their steadfastness depends on remembering the Spirit-inspired teaching about Jesus that they have heard and accepted all along. For it is the Spirit who remains with the faithful and who reminds them of what they have heard *from the beginning.* But clearly John expects that the Spirit works and speaks through individuals who proclaim and teach. This is exactly why the false teachers are such a threat, why he will later warn his readers to "test the Spirits" (4:1-6), and why he continually points to the role of the eyewitnesses and their successors in passing on the truth they have received. While ultimately the Spirit "will teach you all things" (Jn 14:26), the Spirit does so through human beings. Thus, when the Elder writes *you do not need anyone to teach you,* he does not mean that they have never needed any teachers—for he himself was and continues to be their teacher! But they do not now suddenly need new teaching about Jesus, such as the secessionists are offering.

What constitutes a different gospel from the one that they *heard from the beginning* was exactly the source of debate. It is unlikely that the dissidents would say or even agree that they had changed the proclamation. The Elder therefore appeals to his readers' ability to discern, with the aid of the community and by the guidance of the Spirit, whether or not the message they are now hearing conforms to the "Word of life" that they heard initially. The importance of an informed Christian community and the thoughtful understanding of the word of the gospel are foundational to the epistle's appeals and crucial for the health of the church today. John further appeals to his readers to *remain in him,* presumably to remain in God as revealed in the Son. To *remain* implies the maintenance of a stable and vital—but not static!—fellowship with God. In the words of one author, abiding suggests "utter and dependable permanence" (Houlden 1973:82). In this way, we will receive "what he

---

2:26 The NIV helpfully renders the participle *ton planōntōn* with conative force, thus translating *trying to lead you astray.* The author is issuing a warning, not stating a fact.

2:27 It is reading too much into the assertion *you do not need anyone to teach you* to take it as evidence of a democratic community structure that lacked officially appointed

promised us" (v. 25), eternal life.

Here now the first long section of 1 John, which I have called "Walking in the Light: The Fundamental Pattern," comes to a close. In it the author has laid out his view of the life of discipleship as a pilgrimage in which we strive to live within and by the light of God's love, truth and righteousness. Now the imagery shifts somewhat as the Elder introduces and develops the idea that we are the "children of God." The fundamental pattern of what is expected of Christian disciples does not change. But by emphasizing that we are actually bound to God by an intimate relationship—not just as master and disciple, but as parent and child—we gain another angle on understanding the meaning of the life of faith.

□ Remembering Who We Are: The Children of God (2:28—3:24)

One can hardly dispute that the ways in which Christians speak about their understanding of and relationship to God strike non-Christians as ludicrous at best and arrogant at worst. To claim to know God's will surely sounds presumptuous; to claim to know God just a bit preposterous. And the claim that we are *children of God* probably smacks of both. After all, how can people of flesh and blood be children of an eternal being who is Spirit (Jn 4:24)? And why does this status belong to some and not to all? What makes Christians so favored and their claims true, and not mere empty boasting?

The Elder has an answer to these questions. But his answer allows for no smugness on the part of Christians. On the one hand, he affirms to his readers that they are children of God, and so possess immense privileges by virtue of that relationship. But he reminds them that, on the other hand, they have definite responsibilities as God's children. Here is the unequivocal antidote to smugness and arrogance, to any kind of posturing of superiority over non-Christians: it is in our conduct that we make our claims to be God's children believable. The integrity of our lives speaks more loudly than all the claims we can advance.

So in the long section that stretches from 2:28—3:24, the Elder strives

---

human teachers (Brown 1982:106-8, 375-76). But even if the statement here is regarded as a "remarkable exaggeration," the author surely means no more than that the community does not need anyone to teach to them again the essentials of the faith that the dissidents dispute (Kysar 1986:65-66).

both to encourage and to exhort his readers. He encourages them by reminding them of who they are, and he exhorts them by calling them to what they ought to be. But these are scarcely separable for John: *what they are*—God's own children—carries implicit within it *how* they are to live. Who they are prescribes what they ought to be. Put differently, that we are God's children means that we have both privileges and responsibilities.

The privileges given to those who belong to God are confidence and assurance of their status and of God's love for them (2:28—3:3; 19-24). And the responsibility incumbent upon them is to live out that relationship in righteous conduct (3:4-10; 11-18), which points beyond us to the God whom we know. Thus the longer section that focuses on the children of God (2:28—3:24) has within it two subsections (2:28—3:3, 19-24) that deal with the privileges, and two subsections (3:4-10, 11-18) that deal with the responsibilities of being God's children.

The Privileges of the Children of God (2:28—3:3) We come first to a section on the privileges of the children of God. Quite simply, those who are children of God have confidence with God, a theme that is repeated often in the epistle. Such repetition suggests that the readers may well have lacked this confidence, and John wishes to instill in them a vibrant conviction of their salvation. At the least, the return again and again to the theme of assurance points to the beliefs and experience of the author himself. He affirms that in Christ we can indeed have confidence with God, and he has experienced this in his own life.

Confidence with God (2:28-29) In a section that deals with Christian confidence, it may seem odd that the author begins with the exhortation to *continue in him* (that is, in Jesus). By now readers of 1 John

Notes: 2:28 Scholars differ on whether a new unit of thought begins with verse 28, 29 or 3:1. Among those who begin a new unit with verse 29 are Dodd (1946:64-65) and Barker (1982:328); with 3:1, Haas (1972:60, 74), Kysar (1986:69), Smalley (1984:128) and Smith (1991:77). With the NIV and most recent commentators, I suggest that a new subsection begins with verse 28; compare Brown (1982:417-20); Bruce (1970:77); Bultmann (1973:43); Houlden (1973:84); Marshall (1978:164-65); Schnackenburg (1963:162); Stott (1988:120). The transitional phrase *kai nun*, the address to *dear children* (compare v. 18) and the introduction of new subject matter suggest that a new unit of thought begins with 2:28.

The NIV obscures the parallelism between 2:27 and 2:28 by translating the first use of

are familiar with admonitions to "live in him" (2:6) and to let the word of God "remain" in them (v. 24). They can be assured that as a result they will "live forever" (v. 17) and that they will "remain in the Son and in the Father" (v. 24). All these promises and commands use the favorite Johannine term *menein*, "abide." To say that certain things "abide" in the faithful offers them assurance, for "abiding" connotes the permanence of God's blessings.

But if God's blessings are sure and secure, why must believers be *commanded* to "remain" (2:27) and to *continue* (v. 28) in their faith? Do these commands suggest that these readers can lose their status as God's children? Are they in danger of facing God's judgment? These various commands, which urge continued steadfastness, are not intended to frighten the readers or to suggest their inadequacies or failures to abide in Christ. Quite the contrary, these words encourage them to *continue* faithfully in the direction that they have been heading all along. The command admonishes them, but it does so by affirming them in their present course. They have abided; they must continue to do so. Encouragement and exhortation are joined together.

When we continue faithfully in relationship with God, we can be *confident and unashamed* before God when Christ comes. These two adjectives suggest opposing positions: one will either come into God's presence *confident* or one will come in shame. The shame of which the elder speaks is not the shame that believers sometimes imagine that they will or ought to feel in the presence of one who is righteous and pure. It is not embarrassment for those things which we have done wrong. In fact, it is not something that believers are expected to experience at all. Rather, the "shame" that is spoken of here is the disgrace or rejection that *unbelievers* will experience when they come into judgment. And, in

---

menete "remain in him" and the second occurrence as "continue in him." Compare 2:6, 17, "live"; 2:24, 27, "remain" and 2:28, "continue."

The subject of verse 28 is not specified, and *he* can refer either to God or to Christ, here and throughout this section. Most commentators, however, assume that the reference to *his coming* refers to the coming of Christ (though Grayston [1984:95] argues that this phrase refers to God), and take the whole verse as referring to Christ's work in coming to judge. However, it is possible, as Houlden (1973:86) suggests, that believers have confidence before *God* when *Christ* appears. Throughout the epistle believers are said to have confidence with *God* (2:1; 3:19-21; 4:17; 5:14).

context, those who come into such "disgrace" are those who do not "abide."

On the other hand, the confidence that believers have is the boldness to approach God when the coming of Jesus signals divine judgment. The epistle uses two words for Jesus' coming, "appearing" *(phaneroun)* and "coming" *(parousia)*. "Appears" can also be translated "is revealed," suggesting an open and public revelation of Jesus. The word for "coming" *(parousia)* is a technical term in theological language for the return, or Second Coming, of Jesus. It referred in antiquity to the coming of a dignitary or king, with open splendor and honor. To speak of Jesus' "appearing" and public return does not suggest that his first coming was somehow secretive. And yet it is true that there was a hiddenness about it, for not all recognized or received him as the Messiah and Son of God (3:1). In the same way, the world does not recognize Christians to be *children of God* (3:1). But a time is coming when Jesus' true status will be made known publicly. And when Jesus "appears," those who have been faithful, who have "abided," may approach God openly and with great confidence *(parrēsia)*. This term connotes speaking with frankness and openness and points to the privilege of those who are children of God. There is nothing that hinders their relationship with God.

The command ("abide in Christ") functions, then, in two ways. On the one hand, it exhorts readers to continued faithfulness to God as God is made known in Christ. Yet, on the other hand, it is a promise. For it promises to those who continue in their commitment to God that nothing will bring them to shame at the judgment. In this light, the statement *you know that everyone who does what is right has been born of [God]* seems both out of place and possibly even at odds with the promise of

---

2:29 In the statement *if you know that he is righteous,* the *if* does not imply any uncertainty about the righteousness of God (or Christ); compare Smalley (1984:134), "If, as I assume, you know that he is righteous." The if-clause *(if you know that he is righteous)* introduces a second statement that readers will grant because they also agree to the first statement. The Greek *kai,* untranslated by the NIV, can be rendered "also" or "as well." Brown (1982:378): "Once you realize that he is just, you know this as well . . ." (taking *ginōskete,* "know," as indicative, rather than imperative). Again verse 29 is ambiguous concerning to whom the pronouns refer. Clearly *born of him* refers to God, and for this reason some commentators also assert that the statement *he is righteous* refers to God as in 1 John 1:9 (so Dodd 1946:67; Bruce 1970:79; Barker 1981:329; Culpepper 1985:56; Kysar 1986:69; and Stott 1988:122). In the next section, 3:4-10, the likeness of the children of God to the

confidence before God. For who truly "does right" just as *[Christ]* is *righteous?*

Two points must be noted. First, the statement serves to remind readers that righteousness is not simply an intention or feeling, but is manifested in deed and truth, in the moral quality of one's life. Righteousness is the responsibility of those privileged to be God's children. Second, righteous behavior provides confirmation of our relationship with God. Righteous conduct does not make us God's children. Rather, such conduct is the consequence or expression of a relationship that already exists. "To do righteousness" means to "practice it as a pattern of life which comes from one's very nature" (Culpepper 1985:56). Privilege carries with it responsibility. This leads directly to reflections on the designation *children of God.*

The Children of God (3:1-3) Three important ideas are inherent in the assertion that we are God's children: First, it is by God's initiative and power that we are born as the children of God. We do not bring about this relationship any more than a newborn baby caused its own birth and gave itself life.

Second, that God calls us *children of God* inaugurates a reality that will be brought to its fruition at a future time. Again, as a newborn baby lies in its parents' arms, they see it with eyes of hope, possibility and promise. A newborn's birth is not the goal of its existence; its growth and maturity are. Third, that we are God's children is evidence of God's active and creative love for us.

In its translation of 3:1 *(how great is the love...)*, the NIV stresses the amount or extent of God's love for us. But we should not overlook the fact that it is the *way* that God has loved us which shows us how great

---

righteous character of God will be stressed. Other commentators think that *righteous* refers to Jesus as in 1 John 2:1 (Brown 1982:382; Haas 1972:75; Marshall 1978:167 n. 11; Schnackenburg 1963:166; Smalley 1984:133; Smith 1991:75), and since elsewhere Jesus' sinlessness (2:1; 3:5) provides the example for Christian conduct (2:6; 3:16).

The Greek *aischynthōmen* can be taken either as a passive or a middle. If it is read as a passive, "be ashamed," it may reflect a situation in which one is turned away in disgrace and shame (Haas 1972:74; Houlden 1973:86; Marshall 1977:166; Schnackenburg 1963:165; Smalley 1984:131); the middle, "turn away in shame from" suggests a psychological state of shame (Brown 1982:381). But in neither case does it refer to the experience of the faithful believer.

that love is. The kind of love God demonstrates is active and creative love, which "calls" us the children of God. "Calling" means more than naming. It means the inauguration of a relationship, of a reality that can best be pictured by the metaphor of being God's own children. By God's creative act of love, we belong to God as surely and permanently as children belong to their parents. The Elder emphasizes this new relationship when he writes, *And that is what we are!* and *now we are children of God.* We do not simply *look at* a love that is external to us and marvel at its greatness; we *know* a love that resides *within* us. As Westcott comments, God's love is not simply exhibited, it is imparted to us (1966:93).

With the address to his *dear friends* (RSV "beloved"; Gk *agapētoi*) the Elder also emphasizes God's love *(agapē)* for his children and their status as loved by God. And yet there is more to be said. The present fact that we are children of God is contrasted with two things: the lack of present recognition by the world (v. 1), and the future revelation of what we shall be (v. 2).

The world's failure to recognize Christians as God's children could refer to a general lack of understanding on the part of unbelievers as to what Christian life and claims are all about. In the historical context it may also refer specifically to the failure of the dissidents to accept the claims of the Johannine Christians. But the Elder reminds his readers that such lack of recognition should not surprise them, for the world did not recognize Jesus' relationship to God either (Jn 8:19; 15:24; 16:3; even "his own" did not receive him, Jn 1:10). But even as there will come a time of public manifestation and recognition of Jesus (2:28), so there will be a full revelation of what the children of God will be (3:2, fol-

---

3:1 The English *how great* translates *potapēn*, which means "what sort of, what kind of." In context it could suggest either the greatness of God's love ("what great love God gives") or how it has been manifested ("this is what kind of love God gives"). By rendering the simple Greek "has given" as *has lavished*, the NIV again suggests that it is the quantity of God's love that is in view.

In the statement *did not know him*, the pronoun may refer to God (Barker 1981:330; Brown 1982:392; Bruce 1970:87; Houlden 1973:90; Smalley 1984:143) or to the Son (Bultmann 1973:48; Culpepper 1985:57; Dodd 1946:69; Stott 1988:123). In Johannine thought failure to recognize either the Father or the Son would imply a failure to know the other. If the world did not recognize the Son of God, they will surely not recognize the children of God.

lowing the reading in the NIV footnote). If we are God's children *now*, even though the world does not recognize us, what we shall be someday is not known even to us. But since God's children are to reflect God, and since we are promised that when we see God *we shall be like [God]*, we can assume that what we shall be someday brings to fullness and completion the identity that we now cherish as God's own children.

Thus when Jesus appears (2:28) we will be transformed (3:2), and *we shall be like [God], for we shall see [God] as [God] is* (supplying the probable referent "God" for the ambiguous pronoun "him"). Both the Gospel and epistles assert that "no one has ever seen God" (Jn 1:18; 1 Jn 4:12, 20) except the Son, who makes God known. The statement *we shall see him as he is* does not imply that we have somehow been misled in understanding God or that we have been granted an inadequate vision of God in Jesus (Jn 14:8-10), any more than it implies that our present status as *children of God* is somehow inadequate or unsatisfactory. Just as it is true that we shall be changed, so also is it true that a future and new "seeing" of God is promised. We shall see God face to face, even as the Son who is "always at the Father's side" (Jn 1:1-18) sees God. Here John is not so much interested in speculating on what God is like, or precisely what we shall see in our future vision of God. Rather, the accent falls upon knowing God more fully and intimately than is possible for us now.

And when we see God, we shall become like God. This statement in 3:2 is closely linked to the statement in 3:3 that all those who have the hope of seeing God purify themselves, *just as [Jesus] is pure.* Again, the model for our relationship to God is the way in which Jesus relates to God. Jesus has seen God; Jesus is pure as God is pure. There may be

---

3:2 The Greek phrase translated *when he appears* also can be rendered "when it is made known," as the NIV footnote suggests. In this case both uses of "made known" (Gk *phaneroō*) in 3:2 refer to the same thing: the "revealing" of the children of God. The statement would read as follows: "What we will be has not yet been made known. But when it is made known, we shall be like him."

Some take the pronoun *him* in the statement *we shall be like him* to refer to Jesus (Dodd 1946:70; Houlden 1973:91; Marshall 1978:172; Smalley 1984:147; Smith 1991:78; Stott 1988:124); others take it as referring to God (Brown 1982:394; Grayston 1984:101-3; Kysar 1986:74; Schnackenburg 1963:171-72). Again in view of the following section (3:4-10), it is likely that the present passage stresses that we shall be like God.

an implicit reference here to the first "appearing" of Jesus to take away sin (1:7; 3:8). From the beginning to the end of our Christian existence, our hope is in the "appearing" or coming of Christ for us. Our transformation depends on his nature and work: he is pure, and takes impurity away. Thus those who have the hope of Jesus' coming purify themselves, *just as he is pure* (compare 3:5). Hope itself makes us pure, because our hope is trust in Christ's purifying and cleansing work for us.

And so the privilege of being God's children also holds within it the responsibility of living in accordance with the model given to us by God and lived out by Jesus. The privilege also carries with it the promise that someday we shall know the invisible God more fully than we do now, and that when we come to that time, we shall also know ourselves to be pure before him. Responsibility and promise will merge, both fulfilled—not by our own efforts so much as by the work of the One who created us and re-created us in his own image.

Family Likeness (3:4-10) One of the first questions we ask when we hear of the birth of a baby is, "Who does she look like?" Features such as physical appearance, including the color of hair and eyes, facial characteristics, the shape of the mouth or nose, height and build, are given at birth. Later on, as the child grows and begins to reflect its parents' habits of action, speech or attitude, we may speak of a child as "a chip off the old block." Although not all children are simply smaller versions of their parents, it is unusual if there is not something in the physical, emotional or moral makeup of the child that reflects its birth or upbringing.

In this section of the epistle the author develops at greater length the responsibility that falls on the children of God. Quite clearly he expects that the children of God will bear an undeniable resemblance to one whom they claim as their spiritual parent. That resemblance comes to the fore primarily in the sphere of conduct, in the way the child lives out the responsibility summarized in the descriptive phrase *does what is right* (3:7).

In the present passage the Elder makes this point in some of the most emphatic statements in the epistle when he writes that *no one who lives in him keeps on sinning* (3:6) and, more strongly, *[they] cannot go on sinning* (3:9). Because of their absolute and emphatic nature, these statements pose a great challenge to interpretation. (Surveys and discussions of the options are in Brown 1982:412-15; Marshall 1978:178-83; Smalley 1984:159-64; and Stott 1988:134-40.) They seem both overstated and inconsistent with human experience. And to make matters more complicated, 3:4-10 also seems to contradict earlier statements (1:8, 10) that the denial of sin is a sin in itself. In order to unravel this interpretative tangle, I shall first comment on the context and structure of the passage. Then after a verse-by-verse analysis, I shall try to tie together the threads of the discussion to clarify John's intention in the context of the epistle.

The Context and Structure of the Passage Careful attention to the literary context of this passage will reap benefits in interpreting it. We would do well to recall that throughout the epistle the author has tried to encourage his readers and to assure them of their standing before God. If this passage is not to destroy all that he has worked to build, it must instill confidence in his readers. But can absolute statements such as the assertion that the child of God *cannot sin* (v. 9) be heard as encouragement and good news? Yes, they can—*if* we remember that when John reminds his readers that they are the children of God now (3:1), he also directs their hope to the revelation of what they shall be (3:2). Although there is transformation, there is also continuity between present and future. In speaking of the present reality, John anticipates the promised transformation, just as he elsewhere speaks of the reality of eternal life and the outworking of God's final judgment in the present time. The power that is at work in the children of God in the present is the same power that shall transform them at the return of Christ. If they are promised that they will be pure (3:3), in the present they are exhorted to live in anticipation of that promise since the same transforming power is at work in them.

Furthermore, the basis for the hope of the children of God is not their own conduct, but the work of Christ on their behalf. An analysis of the structure of the passage bears out this assertion. The passage consists of two short parallel sections, each of which contains three things: a definition of sin (vv. 4, 8); a statement about the purpose of Christ's work (vv. 5, 8) in light of the definition of sin; and a statement about the implications of Christ's work for the Christian life (vv. 6, 9; Stott 1988:125). The following table illustrates these parallels:

(a) Sin is lawlessness (v. 4)	(a') Sin is of the devil (v. 8)
(b) Christ came to take away sins (v. 5)	(b') Christ came to destroy the devil's works (v. 8b)
(c) No one who lives in Christ keeps on sinning (v. 6)	(c') No one who is born of God will continue to sin (v. 9)

This table shows that Christ's work (b and b') stands in opposition to the power and essence of sin (a and a'). Since believers are those who *live in Christ,* their conduct (c and c') should reflect the work of Christ and its opposition to sin. The work of Christ—begun in his work of taking away sin, yet still to be consummated—anchors John's exhortation to Christian responsibility and his promise of future transformation. With these thoughts in mind, then, we turn to a verse-by-verse analysis of the passage at hand.

Jesus' Sinlessness, Human Sinfulness (3:4-6) While there are, as noted above, two parallel sections (3:4-6; 8-10) that discuss sin, the work of Christ and the implications for the Christian life, each has a distinctive focus. The first subsection draws a contrast between Jesus' sinlessness and human sinfulness.

The character of sin (3:4). John begins with what appears to be a definition of sin when he writes, *everyone who sins breaks the law; in fact, sin is lawlessness.* In describing sin *(hamartia)* as lawlessness or iniquity *(anomia),* he stresses its severity. *Lawlessness* connotes disobe-

Notes: 3:4 The various constructions that the author uses to speak of sinning—*poiein hamartian* (3:4, 8-9); *hamartanein* (3:6, 8-9); and *pas ho hamartanōn* (3:6)—are stylistic variations. The words *breaks the law* and *lawlessness* in the NIV translate cognate constructions in the Greek: *poiein anomia* and *anomia.* A number of commentators take the statement *sin is lawlessness* as providing a definition of sin as "lawbreaking," as disobedience to God's law or to specific commands (Houlden 1973:92; Grayston 1984:104; Kysar 1986:78-79; Stott 1988:126-27). But in the Septuagint *anomia* lacks the specific connotations of "breaking the law" that some try to deduce from its etymology. Iniquity is probably to be understood as end-time rebellion against God (see Brown 1982:399-400; Haas 1972:81; Kysar 1986:78-79; Marshall 1978:176-77; Schnackenburg 1963:185-87; Smalley 1984:155; Smith 1991:83).

3:5 The "appearing" (3:5, 8) of Jesus to take away sins may refer to his Incarnation, his

dience to and rejection of the ways of God. If there are some who tolerate sin as an indifferent matter, this epistle does all in its power to dissuade them from that view.

More specifically, however, *lawlessness* may refer to the lawlessness expected in the last days, the ultimate rejection of God's truth to be manifested in false teaching and immorality (Mt 7:15, 23; 13:41; 24:11-12; 2 Thess 2:3). That meaning of *anomia* fits with John's emphasis that the secessionists are in fact the "antichrists" expected in the last hour (2:18): their sin is not just iniquity, but the iniquity of Antichrist. The fundamental understanding of sin, then, is that it is opposition to the will of God. That opposition need not be manifested in open rebellion or hostility, such as we think of when we consider the animosity to religion that some prominent atheists exhibit. Nor do we have to think of cat-astrophic Armageddons. Indeed, in Johannine thought the antichrists' work is deception (3:7; 4:1), and the primary sin is unbelief. While we might think of unbelief as a passive sin, a sin of omission, the Johannine community was prepared to view it as the supreme manifestation of human sinfulness and rejection of God. Thus the statement *sin is law-lessness* does more than offer a definition of sin. By showing sin for what it is, it encourages renunciation of sin (Smalley 1984:155). For how can sin—opposition to God—be part of the lives of those who vow their allegiance to God?

Jesus' work and nature (3:5). Indeed, those who have vowed their loyalty to God have done so through the mediating work of Jesus Christ. And here John says that Jesus' work is to *take away our sins.* If sin is opposition to God, Jesus' work stands in opposition to sin. If there is

---

death or his entire life. The epistle includes explicit references to Jesus' death as atoning and to his life as exemplary; his entire mission can be characterized as "taking away sin."

Here the NIV follows some manuscripts that read *take away our sins* rather than "take away sins" (RSV). However, the latter form is to be preferred on text-critical grounds. This starker statement also underlines the scope of Jesus' work: because there is no sin in him, he takes away sin.

"Take away sins" may mean either *removing the power of sin,* creating the possibility of freedom from sinning (Bultmann 1973:50; Grayston 1984:105) or *bearing sin by atonement* (Stott 1988:127; Brown 1982:402; Marshall 1978:177; Smalley 1984:156). Compare John 1:29. The epistle's use of the plural *sins* may have in view the plurality of sins committed by individuals, supporting the second meaning (above).

---

opposition between what sin effects and what Jesus effects, then to tolerate or ignore sin in human conduct is to undermine the purpose of Christ's work. It is to cast one's lot with sin, not with God.

For when Christ takes away our sins he takes away sin's consequences—the guilt the sinner has before God—but he also takes way its hold over us, transferring us from darkness to light (3:14) and breaking the power of evil over us (5:18). We are transferred from the sphere of opposition to God to the sphere of life with God. But if we continue in sin, we act as though Jesus had not died for us, as though he had not torn down the walls that trapped us in sin. For although *take away* includes the sense of bearing sin on our behalf, it may mean something closer to "abolish" or "do away with" sin. Jesus' life and death stand in radical opposition to sin and strike at the very heart of the power of sin. Furthermore, to condone or tolerate sin is to negate the life of Jesus as a model of active righteousness for the Christian (2:6).

The implications of Jesus' work and nature for the believer (3:6). Implicit in this section are two important poles in John's thought: On the one hand, he makes repeated references to Christ's role in taking away our sins, thereby stressing the *difference* between the purity and righteousness of Christ and the sinfulness of the believer. On the other hand, though, his emphasis on the present *likeness* between Christ and the Christian cannot be ignored. Both of these must be held together: it is Christ's death alone that purifies (1:7, 9), forgives (1:9) and atones (2:1) for our sin. Thus the statement *no one who lives in him keeps on sinning* depends more on an understanding of what Christ has done for us than it does on what we are able or commanded to do. The Elder's understanding of the Christian life was not developed in observation of the Christian but in perceiving the nature of Christ's life and work.

It follows that the nature of Jesus' work gives shape to the responsibility laid upon his followers, God's children. What is meant, then, by

3:6 In the phrase *seen him* the pronoun refers to Jesus, but *seen* is to be taken, as often in the Johannine writings, metaphorically; there is no fundamental difference between the meaning of "knowing" him and "seeing" him (compare 4:14).

3:8 The NIV renders the plural "works" *(erga)* with a singular *work;* the plural points to all sins as the "works of the devil" (Gk *erga).* The context does not allow further speculation about the nature or scope of the "works of the devil" (contrast Stott 1988:129).

the statement *no one who lives in him keeps on sinning* is quite simple: sin is not the identifying characteristic of those who live *in him.*

Warning Against Deception (3:7) The admonition *do not let anyone lead you astray* serves as a hinge between the sections (3:4-6, 7b-10) that comprise the longer unit (3:4-10). With these words the Elder warns his readers not to be led from the path of following God. They would be led astray if they were to think that righteousness need not find its expression in righteous conduct such as they saw in the life of Jesus himself (2:6; 3:5).

The Work of the Son of God, the Work of the Devil (3:8-10) This second section reiterates the Elder's understanding of sin and righteousness and their relationship to the work of Christ. Although the basic structure of thought parallels that of 3:4-6, the imagery differs. Here John develops the theme of family resemblance and parentage in order to underscore what he has already said about the believer as a child of God who cannot sin (v. 9). Behavior is a test by which one's basic orientation in life may be discerned. Note once more the threefold structure of the passage.

The character of sin (3:8a). In this verse John includes some of the strongest negative statements that those who are sinful are *of the devil.* Both the epistles and Gospel of John frequently speak of being "of" something, a phrase that points to allegiance or orientation. Sinning characterizes the devil, not God, and so those who sin cannot be said to belong to God (3:8, 10). In fact, the Elder writes that the devil *has been sinning from the beginning.* That is, the devil is characterized through and through, and has always been known to human beings, as one who challenged God's standard of righteousness and tempted people to do the same. His identifying characteristic is sin.

Note that the epistle does not say that those who sin are *born* of the devil, which would give a neat parallel to the corresponding phrase *born of God.* But the opposite of *born of God* in Johannine thought is "born

---

From the beginning (ap' archēs) appears with various subjects in 1:1; 2:7, 13-14, 25; 3:11; 2 John 5, 6; and in the Gospel of John at 8:44 and 15:27. Here it has been taken to refer to the beginning of the devil's existence (Bultmann 1973:52 n. 35) or the beginning of human history and sin, that is, the complex of events in Genesis 1—4 (Schnackenburg 1963:189; Brown 1982:406) or, as in the present commentary, "all along" (Brooke 1912:88; Marshall 1978:184 n. 30) or "from the first" (Smalley 1984:169). See the note above on 2:13.

---

of the flesh" (Jn 3:6; Brown 1982:405). All people are created by God (Jn 1:10), but those who come to faith in Christ give evidence that they are also "born of God" (Jn 1:13). A new act of the Spirit's creation has taken place. On the other hand, those who refuse to come to Christ have chosen animosity toward God and allegiance with the devil. They are *of the devil* by virtue of their denial of Christ, deriving their orientation in life not from relationship with and orientation to God but to darkness, evil and sin. Again the Johannine dualism comes to expression. And it is clear from this passage that such dualism is a description not of the way human beings are created but of the choices they make (see Kysar 1986:81).

The work of the son of God (3:8b). If the devil is characterized by sinning, the Son of God is known by his coming *to destroy the devil's work.* This work is sin, for as righteousness characterizes God, the Son of God and the children of God, so sin characterizes the devil and the children of the devil. In fact, it is their sinning that marks them as the devil's children. Not only are the devil's sin and Jesus' sinlessness contrasted but so are their characteristic works: the devil sins, Jesus destroys the devil's works (Stott 1988:129). Jesus tears down the edifice of sin that the devil builds up, and so frees people by transferring them to the realm where they abide in righteousness and in Jesus (3:6, 14).

It is important to note that this transfer is viewed as effective and secure. If believers sin—and it is clear that they do (1:8, 10)—their sin does not indicate that they have temporarily moved into the sphere of darkness. The Elder does not threaten his readers that they are in danger of "losing their salvation," of backsliding or of falling in league with the devil. They are assured that they *are* the children of God. The call comes, then, to live so that the family resemblance will always be manifest. If there is exhortation here, there is also encouragement.

The implications of Jesus' work for the believer (3:9-10). The destruction of the devil's works of sin is so complete that we read a very

---

3:9 For a survey of the meaning of *God's seed* (RSV "God's nature"), see Brown 1982:408-11. His comment is noteworthy: "The exact identification is not so important, so long as we recognize that the author is talking about a divine agency for begetting God's children, which not only brings us into being but also remains and keeps us his children" (p. 411).
3:10 The phrase *This is how we know who the children of God are* in the NIV translates

bold statement in verse 9, *No one who is born of God will continue to sin . . . he* cannot *sin* (or *go on sinning).* Indeed, when Jesus' work both opposes and destroys sin, how can those who are born of God dwell in it? John continues with the explanatory statement that they cannot sin *because God's seed remains in [them].* Exactly what this *seed* is does not receive further explanation, and it has puzzled commentators. Obviously we must take it here in a metaphorical sense. Some have suggested that it means the Holy Spirit; others, the Word of God; and others, that it means both. Perhaps, however, it does not so much symbolize something else, but merely continues the family imagery. As Kysar writes, "God has implanted in Christians that which makes them his children" (Kysar 1986:81; Brown 1982:411; Stott 1988:133-34). And that God's seed *remains* points to the permanence of that work. The seed that God plants cannot be uprooted.

Verse 3:10 takes us back to 3:1-3 and its contrast of the seen and unseen, the known and unknown. In 3:1-3 the Elder asserted that *now we are children of God,* although what we will be *has not yet been made known.* The passage under discussion, 3:4-10, has assumed that just as children have a likeness to their parents, and just as that likeness will and must manifest itself in behavior, so the conduct of the children of God makes it manifest to whom they belong. Specifically, being related to God has two manifestations: righteousness and love. Both are characteristic of God; both are characteristic of the children of God. Moreover, both are and need to be actively expressed, and expressed in a way that conforms to God's standard and to the pattern set by Jesus.

Although the phrase *nor is anyone who does not love his brother* appears to be added almost as an afterthought at the end of verse 10, in fact it is integral to the author's argument. First, the secessionists whom the Elder chides manifest both a lack of righteousness and a lack of love. Thus the statement *anyone who does not do what is right is not a child of God; nor is anyone who does not love his brother* summarizes

---

a Greek phrase that more literally reads "This is how the children of God are manifested." The word for manifested *(phanera)* is a cognate of the word elsewhere translated "appear," used to speak of Jesus' appearing (2:28; 3:2, 5, 8) and of the future appearing of the children of God (3:2; NIV *been made known).*

John's rebuke to the dissidents. It can also be generalized, however, for the author certainly means to say as well that *every* Christian is to be characterized by love and righteousness. Second, those who are related to God as children are also related to each other as brother and sister. Therefore, it is impossible to be part of the family of God and not manifest love toward others in the family. As noted above, the vertical and horizontal relationships of the Christian are always integrally related to each other. Third, the theme of love has now been introduced, and it provides the substance of the rest of the epistle. Thus the argument of the epistle is shifting now from the nature of righteousness, sin and the work of Christ to the nature of love. Here we will see that no less important in understanding love is the person and work of Christ.

Summary: Transforming Power In summarizing this passage, we must first underscore the author's emphasis on Jesus' own righteousness. As the one who is righteous, Jesus effects atonement and forgiveness (2:1). He destroys the unrighteous works of sin and the devil. He provides a model of conduct for the believer (2:6; 3:5). And he will return to complete the work he has begun—to transform us into the image of the God who is pure (3:3). Both the initial manifestation of Christ and his return are spoken of in terms of the effect his work had on sin: in his first coming he took away sin (3:5, 8); in his return (2:28; 3:3) he purifies us.

Clearly, in all this discussion, attention should be focused not on our efforts to become pure or to attain a state of sinlessness, but on what has been done for us to purify us, to transfer us to the realm where righteousness, and not sin, holds sway. God's work through Christ has created a realm where the purifying and transforming power of righteousness, truth and love are operative. And if *now we are children of God* by virtue of that power, *what we will be has not yet been made known.* From beginning to end of our life with Christ, the power at work within and among us is the power of righteousness. That is the privilege and promise that is ours.

Inherent in that promise is an exhortation to righteous conduct. Those *born of God* no longer live without acknowledging God, but are fully aware of the responsibility incumbent upon them as God's children. Their orientation is toward the God who is light (1:5). Their direction in life derives from the character of God. Their responsibility is to live as Jesus did (2:6), in conformity with the character of a God who is righteous, loving and just. Those who say yes to God, whose orientation derives from the will of God, open themselves to God's transforming power. Although God's purifying work is yet to be completed, that transforming power is even now at work among and in those who have been called the children of God.

In short, the statement *No one who is born of God will continue to sin,* and others like it, ought to be heard simultaneously at several levels: First, it orients us to our future hope, a hope that as the children of God we shall yet become more like God. Second, in directing our gaze to our future hope, the statement also assumes that the same power that will remake us at that time is already at work in us. Third, that power is now active in the world because it was manifested by Jesus himself in his work of breaking the grip of sin on us. And finally, in his own life, Jesus exemplified the self-giving love and obedience to God that is the responsibility of God's children as well. If John's statement seems hyperbolic, it is because of his eager anticipation of the blessings of the future age, now being realized through the ministry of Jesus among his followers.

A Rift in the Family (3:11-17) A recent story in a popular magazine gave some suggestions for "How to Heal a Family Feud." It was sprinkled with anecdotes of families torn apart by petty squabbles, carefully nursed grudges, perceived and real hurts, and substantial doses of anger. But there were also stories of happy endings as old wounds were healed and divided families were reconciled. The story included practical advice for bringing about such happy endings—prompt action, candidness, clearing the air, moving ahead step by step and so on. It sounds simple enough. Why is it, then, that rifts and feuds in the family we know as the church are so seldom resolved with such clean and happy endings? And, more to the point for our discussion, why is it that John's own church could not settle its dispute and restore the bonds of fellowship?

To interpret the rift in his church family, the Elder uses the story of the first family and its two sons, Cain and Abel. This story does not have a fairy-tale ending with everyone living happily ever after. But two features of the story make it useful. First, the story of Cain and Abel is not the story of a two-sided feud, like the fabled Hatfields and McCoys, but the account of the evil actions of one brother, Cain. In his evil actions, Cain showed that he was no true brother to Abel. Second, Cain's evil act created such a great rift in the family that we can longer even speak of a break in the family: it created two entirely separate families.

Typical of the epistle, the contrast between these families is spelled out in absolute terms. Abel represents the children of God, who are characterized by righteousness (v. 12), life (vv. 12-15), love and pity (vv. 13-14, 17), righteous conduct (vv. 16-18) and fellowship (vv. 13-15). Cain represents the *children of the devil* (v. 10), who are known by evil (v. 12), death and murder (vv. 12-15), hate (vv. 13-14, 17), unrighteous conduct (vv. 16-18) and hostility to the children of God (v. 13). These descriptions do not mean that Abel never did anything wrong or that Cain never did anything right. Rather, John's dualistic language points both *descriptively* and *prescriptively* to the identifying characteristics of those in the light and those in the darkness. John now picks up one of these identifying marks as he speaks of the children of God as those who are to love each other.

Disobeying the message (3:11-13) The command to love each other is *the message you heard from the beginning* (compare 2:7, 10). Indeed, it was given by Jesus himself (Jn 13:34; 15:12, 17). But earlier the Elder had summed up "the message we have heard from him" (1:5) as "God is light." There is clearly a close connection between these statements (Haas 1972:87). For love originates with God. Those who are then *born of God* and live in the light must and will reflect God's love to others in the family (2:9-10), just as they reflect his righteousness (3:4-10).

Cain provides a negative example at two points. First, he does not manifest love for his brother, and so shows that he belongs to the world and the sphere of death (3:12-14). But even worse, he is guilty of an act that robbed his brother of *life;* he is a murderer (v. 15). And although

Notes: **3:11** Smalley (1984:181-82) argues that verse 11 ends the previous section; but most commentators take it as introducing what follows. Stott (1988:143) suggests that 3:10 prepares the reader for the change of subject from righteousness to love, but love is not so much a new subject as it is an expression of righteous behavior. The style of introducing

this is a story about two brothers, it is really Jesus, and not Abel, who provides the positive example for the Johannine Christians (v. 16). For where Cain hated, Jesus loved and gave the command to love. Where Cain murdered, Jesus granted fullness of life, for he himself is life (1:2; 3:16; 5:11-12, 20; John 10:10; 11:25; 14:6).

But the secessionists' actions of false teaching and creating schism in the church mirror those of Cain, not of Jesus. For those who follow them and their teaching leave the sphere of life for the sphere of death (3:14). The Johannine Christians are to be on their guard against those who would rob them of life. But they must also take heed lest in their own actions they fail to live out the love that was commanded and modeled by Jesus himself (compare v. 16).

Does the Elder's choice of Cain and Abel, a pair of *brothers,* to illustrate the hostility of the secessionists indicate that he still regards them as "brothers" to the Johannine Christians? Some commentators argue that *brother* really means neighbor, whether that neighbor is in the world or the church (Bultmann 1973:28-29; Schnackenburg 1963:195). This seems unlikely, for it contradicts the epistle's family imagery (3:4-10), where children belong either to one family or the other and are therefore siblings to those in that family. Cain and Abel are chosen because Cain should have acted as a brother: with love and pity. But instead he showed that he was no true brother at all, not a child of God (3:12, *his own actions were evil;* compare 3:6, 9).

Likewise, the secessionists may have appeared to be brothers, but that was a lie whose truth in the end was exposed (2:18-23). Cain, in fact, *belonged to the evil one.* In his behavior he showed himself at enmity with God. But he was no puppet of the evil one. Cain murdered Abel not because of any predetermined role or inescapable urge but because *his own actions were evil and his brother's were righteous.* Children of God will reflect the righteousness of God; those who are not children of God reflect the sinfulness that characterizes the realm of evil. As Jesus

new but closely related thoughts is typical of 1 John (see, for example, 3:24 and 4:1; 5:5 and 6).

3:12 In Jewish literature and the New Testament, Cain represents those who rebel against God; compare Jude 11. There are numerous references in Brown (1982:442-43) and Grayston (1984:110).

said, "A tree is recognized by its fruit. . . . The good [person] brings good things out of the good stored up in him, and the evil [person] brings evil things out of the evil stored up in him" (Mt 12:33, 35). While for John it is inevitable that one's actions will manifest one's inner character, those actions are neither predetermined nor automatic. Cain made a choice: he disobeyed God. And he forsook his responsibility to his brother.

The same is true of the secessionists. In breaking fellowship with the Johannine church and separating themselves from the community, they have manifested what the author calls "hatred"—a strong term indeed! Hatred connotes fundamental opposition to the values and commitments of others (Grayston 1984:68, 112; Smalley 1984:187). This is the way the world responds to God's children. But the world's hostility should not surprise the Johannine Christians (v. 13). They would surely remember the words of Jesus that the world will hate his followers just as it hated him (Jn 15:19-21).

Sometimes this passage is understood to imply that if Christians were to live truly in obedience to God's commands, the church would feel the full wrath of the hatred of the world. So Christians begin to wonder what is wrong if they are not being persecuted. But the Elder does not say that the *more* righteous we are and the *more* we live as the children of God, the *more* the world will hate us, as if the quantity of our obedience determined the world's response to us. Rather, he states a simple fact: there is hostility between the world and thje children of God. They have conflicting loyalties and values (2:15-17), and the world attempts to dissuade Christians from their commitments (2:26; 3:7). The challenge to the present-day reader is to discern when the church is truly experiencing the hostility of the world. Not everything that the church undertakes necessarily comes from God, nor does all opposition to the church necessarily come from evil. While the world's hostility is to be expected, it is not to be made a badge of the quality of our Christian life. True assurance of who we are comes in a more positive way.

Hearing the Message (3:14-15) The Johannine Christians can be

---

3:14 The statement *because we love our brothers* explains on what grounds *we know*

assured of their relationship with God by their continuing love for each other. Love for each other shows that we have *passed from death to life*, because it shows that we have experienced God's love for us, and understood the character of God. Love also shows that we are following the model of Jesus' own self-giving love and living in obedience to Jesus' commands. Love is an *expression* of the transforming power of God at work in us and in the church. And just as love for others is the expression of knowledge of the God who is love (4:16), so hate expresses the death and darkness that come from lack of knowledge of God.

Jesus' Example: Love That Brings Life (3:16) By now the reader is well aware that love is a central theme and concern of 1 John. But with 3:16 we come to the first of several statements in the epistle that state explicitly, *This is . . . what love is* (compare 4:8-10, 16). And it is the voluntary self-giving of Jesus to others, in life and death, that constitutes the epitome of God's love (4:9-10). Not only do we see the fullness of God's love in Jesus' death, we see also the essence of love itself.

With the statement *This is how we know what love is,* John points to two things important for us to remember. Jesus' voluntary giving of life is both an *example* for us to emulate and a *revelation* of the extent of God's love (Smalley 1984:194; Stott 1988:147). As an example, Jesus shows us that true love is concrete and active, not merely felt or thought, but lived out. As a revelation of God's love, Jesus shows us that God was active in sending the Son so that we might know God, have life and live within the circle of love. But in saying that the sending of the Son is a revelation of God's love, we do not mean that we admire it as we might a display in a museum or art gallery. Nor does God put the Son on parade as we might celebrate a hero, president or winning sports team or figure, so that we can cheer and applaud.

God's love is not simply a thing to be admired. It is, rather, the power that transfers those who have faith from death to life, from the realm of hatred to love. Imagine that a friend is standing at the end of a pier and throws a life-preserver out in the water. If he then turns to you and says, "See how much I love you?" the action will seem odd at best. If you are

(oidamen; Houlden 1973:98; Marshall 1978:191 n. 11; Smalley 1984:189), not on what grounds *we have passed from death to life* (Bruce 1970:95-96).

safe on the pier, how does your friend's action embody love? But if you are drowning in the water and your friend throws you the life-preserver and pulls you to safety, you would not need idly speculate about his motivation, and he would not need to say, "I love you." Because your life has been saved, you know you are loved (see Marshall 1978:193). Similarly, for people to know of the reality and greatness of God's love they must experience it as a love that is active *for them.*

Jesus' Action: Life That Brings Love (3:17) Jesus' death and love creates the community of life and love. Those within that community ought to manifest a love for others that serves the end of nurturing community (v. 16). And one does not strengthen community by speech alone, but by *actions and in truth.*

But what is self-giving love? To lay down one's life for another sounds noble and heroic, but this concept is often misunderstood and misused. To tell the woman or child who is being abused that they are manifesting "self-giving" or sacrificial love is bad advice and poor theology. Sacrificial love that models itself after Jesus' example does not enable the destructive behavior of others, but encourages them in actions that lead to love and life, and to healing and wholeness.

We may note at least four features of Jesus' self-giving love as we seek to implement truly sacrificial love in our relationships. Jesus *voluntarily* chose to lay down his life. He had a choice, and he could have chosen differently. Second, the results of his death are *life-giving* for others (Jn 10:11, 15, 17-18). Third, true love is always accompanied by *truth* and never by deception or lies (3:7-10). It lives fully in the light, and does not have to hide its actions. Fourth, we are to give *out of our abundance,* from what we have, to those who have not. Jesus gave the life he had from the Father to be our life: he gave from his strength to our weakness. Self-giving love gives out of what we are and have to the weakness or lack of others.

Specifically, the Johannine Christians who have *material possessions (echein ton bion tou kosmou)* are instructed to give to those who are *in need (echein chreian).* Although this may seem far less demanding and heroic than the willingness to sacrifice one's life for another, it is

---

3:17 In the rhetorical question, *How can the love of God be in him?* the phrase *love of God* can refer either to human love for God, God's love for human beings or God's kind of love. On analogy with verse 15, which states that no murderer has eternal life in him,

surely difficult enough! It is sobering to be reminded that the average American church member gives about 2-3 per cent of their annual income to various charities and causes—including the church. The principle of conduct John gives here is simple: we ought to be willing to give up what we have in order to enrich the lives of others. And while it is commendable when this is done out of a free and generous spirit, it is more important to do the right thing than to wait for the right motivation. Often willingness and motivation to do right can be nourished by the actual action of doing what is right.

Since John has just laid down a principle for conducting ourselves in love toward one another, we come back to the question with which we opened this section: Why is it that John's own church could not settle its dispute and restore the bonds of fellowship? In fact, the choice of Cain and Abel portrays in the strongest possible imagery the dualism between death and life and between hate and love. The unremitting dualism and the absolutely negative terms in which the Elder interprets the actions of the secessionists is a bit disconcerting.

But it is important to remember that we do not know everything we would like to know. For example, we do not know what measures the Elder or his adherents took to bring the secessionists back to the fold. This letter was probably written after the break, since it seems to look back and interpret what has happened and why it happened. What went on before this point is not known to us. Clearly the Elder would not have considered compromising his understanding of the person and work of Jesus. But what else he might have done to try to heal the rift, or how he acted, or what was said, remains lost to us. By the time this letter was written the categories are fixed in the Elder's mind, and he speaks in absolute, dualistic terms. It is important to remember how "dualism" and dualistic language functions. When the author speaks of the truth, life and love of the church, he refers not to the church's moral superiority so much as to its commitment to these realities and to the one who ultimately is truth, life and love. And it is incumbent upon the children of God to be as persistent in love as God was in seeking each of them out.

---

it is probably best to take *love of God* here as "God's own love" (subjective genitive), which naturally also implies that it is God's kind of love (see Brown 1982:450).

The Confidence of the Children of God (3:18-24) Probably no human relationship is so characterized by boldness and confidence as that of young children before their parents. With complete trust a child comes to a parent and asks for help, for attention, for companionship. When my daughter comes to me with a request, my answer is sometimes "yes," sometimes "not now" or "later," and sometimes even "no." She knows that at times I may refuse a request, but she also knows that she can come again and again and have her needs tended to, her requests granted, and find a friend who will spend time with her.

Precisely that relationship of children to their parents, that relationship of implicit trust, of confidence and willingness to ask again and again, characterizes the stance of the believer before God. Here are strong words of assurance to believers who doubt the status of their own relationship with God.

An Unsettling Lack of Confidence (3:18-20) This next short section begins with a pastoral exhortation that Christians live out their love. In the contrast between *words* or *tongue* on the one hand and *actions* and *in truth* on the other, the Elder urges his readers to live in conformity to what he knows to be *the truth,* the revelation of God's love in Jesus himself (Kysar 1986:85).

In verse 19 there is an implicit promise that believers can *know that [they] belong to the truth,* a promise closely linked to the exhortation of

Notes: 3:18 The NIV translates a singular "action" *(ergon)* with a plural *actions,* which can be misleading. The phrase *en ergō* implies living out our commitments.

3:19 The link between verses 18 and 19 is grammatical as well as logical. *This . . . is how we know (en touto)* of verse 19 looks back to the command of verse 18 (Bruce 1970:98; Brown 1982:454; Culpepper 1985:72; Dodd 1946:90; Houlden 1973:101; Smalley 1984:200; Schnackenburg 1963:201; Stott 1988:148-49). Barker (1981:337) and Kysar (1986:86) think that the *this* refers to verse 20, *God is greater than our hearts.*

The Greek *emprosthen* (NIV *in his presence;* RSV "before him") is taken by some commentators in a forensic sense, to refer to judgment by God (Brown 1982:455; Bultmann 1973:56 n. 59; Smalley 1984:201-2), and by others to refer more generally to any situation in which one feels lack of confidence before God, perhaps particularly in times of prayer (Houlden 1973:102; Marshall 1978:149; Schnackenburg 1963:202 n. 7). The second sense probably includes the first (Culpepper 1985:72). The three prepositions used in 3:19-24 to speak of being "before God" *(emprosthen* [3:19]; *pros* [3:21; compare 5:14] and *enōpion* [3:22]) have no substantive difference in meaning.

The verb translated *set . . . at rest (peisomen)* can mean "persuade" or "reassure." The difference is not very great, since the point of "persuading" our hearts is to reassure ourselves in the presence of God.

Most commentators understand *heart* to refer to what we call "conscience," but it may

verse 18 to *love . . . with actions and in truth.* Love for one another gives us assurance that we *belong to the truth,* because love is a visible manifestation that we know the God who is truth and love (4:8, 16). Because we know that we are of the truth, *we set our hearts at rest in [God's] presence.* The Elder previously has spoken of coming to God in confession (2:1), of having confidence before God at the coming of Christ (2:28) and at the judgment (4:17), and later he will speak of the confidence believers have with God when they pray (5:14-15). In the present passage, however, John does not have in view a specific time or instance when we come into God's presence, for whenever believers come before God, they come with confidence rather than fear (compare 4:17-18), anxiety or self-incrimination. Confidence before God springs from our relationship with God, and that kind of confidence is as natural in God's children as the confidence of children in their human parents.

While the epistle promises that we can have assurance that we belong to the truth, as evidenced by our deeds of love, there may be times when we feel we have not lived this out, and so our hearts incriminate and condemn us (3:19b). In those times, the Elder reminds us, we are to remember that God is *greater than our hearts, and he knows everything.* The twin affirmations that *God is greater than our hearts* and *knows everything* imply that the human heart is not the final standard of judgment or mercy: rather, God is, and God's power keeps believers from

also refer to the emotional aspect of human affections and feelings (Brown 1982:456).

3:20 Some commentators see this verse not as a promise but as a warning about God's judgment. For if our own hearts, with their limited knowledge, warn us of our failures, how much more does God who knows everything know our sins (Grayston 1984:115). On this view, the verse is intended to quicken sluggish consciences, to drive one to repentance and to foster obedience to God's commands. But this interpretation seems to direct the verse to the dissidents, for the problem with which the Elder is dealing is not *laxity* in his own congregation but the *defection* of certain members of the church, which itself points to their failure to love.

The interpretation of verse 20 depends on two factors: What does it mean that God knows everything? How is God greater than our hearts? *[God] knows everything* may mean that because God knows all God forgives all (Kysar 1986:87; Schnackenburg 1963:203; Stott 1988:150); or that because God knows all, God's judgment is to be feared (Grayston 1984:115-16); or that because God knows all God can be more objective in judgment (Brown 1982:458; Dodd 1946:90; Marshall 1978:198 n. 7; Smalley 1984:203). Similarly, some commentators take *greater* to mean "greater in judgment" while others take it to mean "greater in mercy" or "forgiveness." For *greater (meizōn),* a favorite Johannine word, compare John 1:50; 4:12; 5:20, 36; 8:53; 10:29; 13:16; 14:12, 28; 15:13, 20; 19:11; 1 John 3:20; 4:4; 5:9; 3 John 4. One need not supply either "judgment" or "mercy." See Smith 1991:96.

the onslaughts of the world. God's *greater* power insures the faithfulness of the Johannine Christians (compare Jn 10:29; 14:28; 1 Jn 4:4; 5:9). They need not fear even if their hearts were to condemn them, for God knows those who belong to the flock. The ultimate basis of our relationship to God and confidence with God is not the steadfastness of Christians but the greatness of God. As Jesus said, "My Father, who has given them to me, is greater than all; no one can snatch them out of my Father's hand" (Jn 10:29).

We may see here the Elder's concern to strengthen discouraged individuals in the face of challenges hurled at them by the secessionists. Despite the secessionists' claims to *belong to the truth,* John argues that when their claim is tested against the standard of genuine love, they come up short. The Johannine Christians need not be anxious that it may in fact be their own claim to know God that is defective: they can know that they belong to the truth, because they have committed themselves to loving the children of God by remaining steadfast in fellowship.

Reassuring Confidence in Prayer (3:21-22) But, in fact, the Elder expects that their hearts will not condemn them. He does not want Christians to dwell in the realm of anxiety and doubt, but rather to be assured of their relationship with God and so to be instilled with confidence. The words *if our hearts do not condemn us* do not imply that Christians never fail or fall short, much less that they are unaware of such failings. Indeed, the necessity of confession (1:8, 10) implies their full awareness of sin. But sin is no barrier to our having confidence if we come to God in confession, and even at those times, when our assurance is perhaps lowest, we can come confidently, since our advocate is Jesus Christ himself (2:1-2).

Just as boldness and confidence characterize children who make requests of their parents, so too boldness and confidence are to distinguish the children of God as they approach God in prayer. The Elder speaks of this boldness in the strongest possible language when he states that we *receive from [God] anything we ask.* Similar promises are found in 5:14-15 and in the Gospel of John (14:13; 15:7, 16; 16:23, 26). Typically these promises have some sort of qualification: asking in Jesus' name (Jn 14:13; 16:23, 26) or according to God's will (1 Jn 5:14), abiding in Jesus (Jn 15:7, 16) and keeping the commandments (1 Jn 3:21). In some sense, certain "conditions" must be met for us to be given *anything we ask*. But what is the nature of these conditions?

What all these "conditions" (praying in Jesus' name, doing God's will, abiding in Jesus) have in common is that they are expressions in the life of the believer of an already existing relationship of love between God and the believer. They are not conditions that one must strive to meet with the hope of getting a hearing with God. Thus to pray "in Jesus' name" means that prayers are offered through the mediation or intercession of Jesus (2:1-2). Prayer according to God's will (5:14) is prayer that understands what is pleasing to God (3:20) and makes its petitions accordingly. The present verse assures us that our prayers are answered *because we obey his commands and do what pleases him*. And by now it is apparent in 1 John that "obeying his commands" is not a prerequisite to fellowship with God, but rather the manifestation of that fellowship.

We do not come to God as strangers pleading for special favors, but as those whom God calls "children." Just as requests and petitions comprise much of the language of children to their parents, so petitionary prayer constitutes much of the address of Christians to their heavenly Father. When we are told that we *receive . . . anything we ask*, we are not promised that every item on our wish list will be granted to us. We are, rather, reminded of the intimate bond that we have with God, a bond that makes it possible for us to bring our petitions to God at all. For petition does not bring about intimacy, confidence and trust; rather, intimacy and trust elicit petition. We can bring our requests to God with confidence because we indeed belong to the truth: we belong to God.

Confidence from Obeying God's Command (3:23-24) In verse 22 we read that we receive what we ask for in prayer because *we obey [God's] commands and do what pleases [God]*. The plural *(commands)* of verse 22 now becomes a singular *(command)* in verse 23, but the one command has two aspects: to believe in Jesus and to love one another. Throughout the epistle the Elder has separated these commands, sometimes emphasizing the command to love one another (2:8; 3:11-18; 4:7-8, 19-21; 5:1-5) and sometimes the command to believe in Jesus (2:22-25; 4:1-3, 13-15; 5:5-12). But love and belief are not two separate commands one must keep in order to be a child of God. They are two different expressions of the indwelling of God in us, for God is love and as perfect love sent Jesus the Son to give us life. Thus the two commands are really one, since the pre-eminent expression of God's love for us is the giving of Jesus Christ to us. (The implicit relationship between belief and love is developed at greater length in 4:7-21.)

When John writes that *those who obey his commands live in him, and he in them,* he does not mean that obedience to the commands is a prerequisite to God's dwelling with us. One cannot justly claim a relationship to God without that obedience, for a child of God will naturally seek to do what pleases God. But becoming a child of God does not come about by our efforts; the very image of being born of God suggests otherwise. The relationship is established first, by God; our part is manifested in obedience to God's commands. Thus there is mutual indwelling: we can be said to live out our lives in the sphere of obedience and love for God, and in turn God cherishes, protects and lives with us.

Further evidence of God's presence with us is the Spirit, which has been given to us. Here John is not likely referring to an "inner testimony" or conviction that the Spirit gives us, a sort of feeling that we are indeed in relationship with God. To reduce the Spirit's witness to a purely internal experience or feeling would grant too much ground to the secessionists, who could easily make the same claim. The Elder's way of writing implies that the Christian belief that God dwells in them can be verified (Houlden 1973:106-7). As always in 1 John, the author points to the tangible manifestation and visible expression of claims to know God. As will become clear in the following chapter, we know that we have the Spirit because only God's spirit inspires true confession of Christ (4:1-6) and empowers us to love one another (4:7-21). Because the Spirit is present with us, we keep the command of verse 23: *to believe in the name of his Son, Jesus Christ, and to love one another.*

□ Walking in the Light: Belief and Love (4:1—5:12)
With 4:1 the epistle shifts its focus somewhat. The previous section (2:28—3:24) dealt with what it means to be God's children. Now a long section on belief and love begins. To be sure, belief and love are both identifying marks of the children of God. But the emphasis here will not fall so much on how these characterize God's children as it will on how God works to bring about true confession and true love. This long

section begins and ends with a subsection on belief (4:1-6; 5:6-12). In between is one subsection that deals with love for each other (4:7-12) and two (4:13-21; 5:1-5) that interweave both themes.

Together the threads of love and faith weave the tapestry of Christian life. But these two threads are not chosen at random nor are they independent of each other. Rather, they are intimately related, for it is through the Son that God's love is manifested (4:10-11), and in this Son the readers are called to have faith (4:2-3, 14-15; 5:1, 5-12). We can expect, then, that the threads of love and faith shall reappear and cross over each other many times and that, as they do, the textures and colors will deepen and become richer. But we turn, first, to a passage that exhorts the faithful to be alert to the dangers of deception from these false teachers.

Discerning the Spirits (4:1-6)   My husband and I are birdwatchers. No serious "birder" would be without a good field guide or two. A field guide is simply a book with pictures and descriptions of birds and their chief identifying characteristics, including size, coloration, voice, range, habitat and so on. With a field guide and a little practice, one can become adept at identifying literally hundreds of birds.

What this passage gives us is in its own way a "field guide" to identifying or discerning "spirits." Specifically, it calls attention to two distinct "field marks" of various spirits: first, what they say or teach; second, who hears or accepts their teaching. That seems straightforward enough. With this knowledge in mind, we ought to be able to venture forth to spot and identify a variety of spirits, simply by checking each species against our guide. Why, then, does it seem that so many people cannot see the spirits for what they are and fall prey to all varieties of heresies, misinterpretations of Scripture, cults and fads? And even when we can discern truth from error and determine that a particular teaching, person or group is wrong, what are we to do? Is it enough not to follow that teaching? Are we, as individuals or as a church, to do something more than resist perversions of the truth, as important as that is? Such questions are not easily answered. After a look at the content of the passage under consideration, we will suggest some guidelines—and call attention to some of the difficulties—in this matter of discerning the spirits.

To understand John's instruction to *test the Spirits,* we need to place it in the context of Johannine church life. People met in houses in groups of about twenty to thirty people, for worship and fellowship (compare 2 Jn 10). These scattered communities did not have immediate access to authoritative figures like the Elder, and communication with them was not always easy. Apparently the Elder sent emissaries to communicate with the churches (3 John 5-8), sometimes carrying letters such as these epistles. These congregations had been glad to welcome the Elder's traveling ambassadors. But now there were also "false prophets" who, like the emissaries of the Elder, would have claimed to speak the truth under the inspiration of the Spirit. And, finally, there were also various itinerant philosophers who traveled in hopes of a hearing and a place to stay. In light of this complex situation, John is anxious to provide his readers with criteria against which claims to truth and inspiration could be tested.

Spirit-inspired Prophets (4:1) Clearly the claim to be inspired by the Spirit can and must be tested, for the claim to have the Spirit is not proof that one does. Here *spirit* has been variously taken to refer to the *spirit* that inspires the prophet, to the *person* who is inspired or to the *message* delivered by the prophet. Obviously the three are related, for in testing a person's words one is actually testing whether or not that person speaks by divine guidance. In light of the rest of the passage two things emerge: First, the author believes that individual persons are inspired or led to confess or deny Christ by *spirits,* some reality beyond the human individual. Second, ultimately there are only two spirits: God's Spirit, also called the Spirit of truth because it guards and inspires truth (4:2, 6); and the spirit of antichrist, which inspires falsehood, and especially false confession of Christ (vv. 3, 6). The Elder's readers are not

---

Notes: **4:1** *World* does not have a neutral meaning here (Haas 1972:104; Marshall 209 n. 108; Schnackenburg 1963:219) but carries the connotation of antithesis to truth and to God (Brown 1982:491; Smalley 1984:220).

4:2 *This is how (en toutō)* refers forward to the content of the christological confession stated in this verse.

In Greek the word *you know (ginōskete)* can be either indicative (statement of fact; NIV) or imperative (command; KJV). With the NIV it is best taken here as indicative. The Elder assures his readers that they can discern the spirits; after all, they have "an anointing" (2:27) that confirms to them "what you have heard from the beginning" (2:24) (Brown 1982:491; Smalley 1984:220).

The NIV translates *homologeō* (vv. 2-3) as "acknowledge" (compare RSV "confess"). This

to believe every claim to be divinely inspired or to have a prophetic message, but are rather to *test the spirits,* to discern whether a message is the truth that comes from God.

Such testing is necessary because *many false prophets have gone out into the world.* While "prophet" in the Pauline literature refers to a specific function within the church (Rom 12:6; 1 Cor 12:10; 14:1-5, 29-33; Eph 4:11), the Johannine epistles refer more broadly to all of those who left the church as *false prophets,* because they carry with them testimony that claims to be spirit-inspired. That is exactly the point: *all* persons speak by the inspiration of one spirit or another (Brown 1982:489). Now it falls to the community to discern which spirit guides the teaching of the various individuals whom they encounter. The church must exercise discernment, then as now, for truth and error are not always easily distinguished. They do not exist disembodied, but come to us in the shape of real persons with whom we share a variety of relationships. Precisely because "testing the spirits" entails dealing with other persons, perhaps even professed Christians, who claim to be guided by the Spirit, we must exercise care and humility in discerning the truth.

Spirit-inspired Confessions (4:2) The Elder now offers one test by which the Spirit's inspiration may be discerned, and that is the test of the substance of one's teaching; specifically, one's teaching about Jesus Christ (vv. 2-3). The emphasis on true confession indicates that John is not talking about demon possession or ecstatic utterances or prediction of the future but about accepting the affirmations about Jesus that have been handed down in the community. This is not a new test, nor does the author expect the church to do anything new in exercising discernment. But he reminds them that the stakes are high. In the bal-

---

is the same word found at 1:9; 2:23; 4:3, 15; 2 John 7. It implies both the recognition of the true identity of Jesus and the open acknowledgment of faith in him (Smalley 1984:221).

The setting of the confession may be worship or perhaps baptism (Brown 1982:504-5; Houlden 1973:107-8; Smalley 1984:221), although "confession" was probably not limited to such occasions. Despite the conjectures of several scholars, there is no evidence of impressive ecstatic utterances in the community (Barker 1981:340; Houlden 1973:107-9; Marshall 1978:204). As Brown (1982:489) notes, *all* have a spirit. The issue is not, as in Corinth, the discernment of a variety of charisms, including the prophetic gift, but the recognition of the two spirits of truth and error as they are manifested in the lifestyles and confessions of various persons.

The statement of 4:2 has been read at least four ways: (1) *Every spirit which confesses*

ance hang truth and error about the first commandment and the ultimate question of faith: knowledge and worship of the one true God. For denial of Jesus would be tantamount to worshiping a false god, since only through Christ is knowledge of the true God mediated (5:21).

But the problem that the author has to deal with is not a blatant rejection of Jesus; it is a distortion of the acknowledgment that *Jesus Christ has come in the flesh.* Exactly what is at stake in that acknowledgment has been the source of much debate (see the footnote for discussion of options). The formulation found here clearly echoes traditional language, such as that of the statement of John 1:14, "The Word became flesh." This affirmation was central to the Johannine community's understanding of Jesus, and it may well be that "Jesus Christ Incarnate" had become virtually a credal way of speaking about Jesus. Several ideas would be bound up in that confession. First, in Jesus, people came to know not just a rabbi from Nazareth but the Word of God. Second, Jesus was a human being of flesh and blood. Third, this human being, the Word made flesh, revealed God to us. Finally, the one who "comes down from heaven and gives life to the world" (Jn 6:33) did so by giving his "flesh" in death (Jn 6:51).

What is difficult to determine is what aspect of this confession—if any—was being denied by the schismatics. Did they reject this whole formulation? Did they question the deity of the Word? Did they perhaps challenge the true humanity of the Incarnate One? Could most of those who left the church have given a clear accounting of the difference

---

[or acknowledges] that Jesus Christ has come in the flesh (KJV, RSV, NIV, NASB, NEB; Houlden 1973:107). This translation supplies *that* to the Greek text and translates the participle *(elēlythota)* as a perfect *(has come),* thus suggesting that what is at stake is a denial of the Incarnation. (2) "Every spirit which confesses Jesus Christ come in the flesh" (Brown 1982:492-93; Grayston 1984:121; Smalley 1984:222-23). This is the most literal translation; it makes "Jesus Christ come in the flesh" the whole object of the verb "confess." (3) "Every spirit which confesses Jesus Christ as come [or "as having come"] in the flesh" (Marshall 1978:205), stressing the nature of the coming (see Jn 2:7). (4) "Every Spirit which confesses Jesus as the Christ having come in the flesh" (Dodd 1946:100-101; Stott 1988:157-59). Behind this translation lies the hypothesis that the dissidents viewed the heavenly Christ as coming (temporarily) upon the earthly Jesus, so that John would be insisting that Jesus is the Messiah-come-in-the-flesh. This last option supplies the most to the Greek and depends most heavily on a particular theory of the heresy of John's opponents. Options two and three do not differ greatly; both provide a neater parallel to the simpler formulation of verse 3. Smalley's translation, "Every spirit who acknowledges Jesus Christ, incarnate" highlights the parallel between verses 2 and 3. The first option may unduly shift the focus

between the Elder's Christology and their own?

We find two clues to answering these questions in other passages in the epistle and from the mere fact that these false prophets have left the church. First, other passages in the epistle stress the importance of Jesus' death and the atonement that it makes for sin (1:7; 2:1-2; 4:9-10, 14). Only through the Son does God give life (5:11-12). In other words, while the Elder is concerned that his readers understand who Jesus is, he also wants to remind them of the salvation that is theirs as they profess commitment to Jesus. Second, we know that some people have deserted the Elder's congregation. To leave the fellowship that Jesus called into being is to put oneself outside of the sphere of light, life and truth. To reject the necessity of his atonement for sin likewise manifests that one remains in darkness. In the end, to do either is to "deny Jesus." Thus while the confession "Jesus Christ Incarnate" encapsulates John's understanding of Jesus, in the present context it may be used to remind the readers of the salvation that comes through Jesus and to exhort them to faithfulness to him.

Spirit-inspired Allegiance (4:3) And so John paraphrases the longer statement that one must acknowledge *that Jesus Christ has come in the flesh* (4:2) with the simpler formula that one must *acknowledge Jesus* (v. 3). Such a restatement makes it clear that what John ultimately seeks is faith in a person, the Incarnate Christ, and not faith in a doctrine, even the doctrine of the Incarnation (Smalley 1984:223). "Acknowledgment" (NIV) or "confession" (RSV) of Jesus means allegiance to him. It

---

to the fact of the Incarnation, which is not under debate in the epistle. It is not clear that the dissidents would have denied the statement of verse 2, but in the Elder's view, they were not confessing Jesus (v. 3) who, in Johannine tradition, was the "Incarnate One." Compare 2 John 7; John 1:14.

4:3 There are two textual variants in verse 3. Although Brown (1982:494-96) argues at great length for the variant reading *lyei* ("annuls"), there are good reasons for accepting the better-attested reading *mē homologei* (see the long note in Marshall [1978:207 n. 11]). With respect to the second variant, virtually all scholars accept the shorter reading *Jesus*, since the others are easily explained as scribal additions to it.

In the phrase translated *the spirit of the antichrist*, the word *spirit* is missing in the Greek. Some commentators suggest that this lacuna permits a "generalizing interpretation" (Westcott 1883:143; Marshall 1978:208 n. 12) along the lines of the NEB, "This is what is meant by 'Antichrist' "; or that it deliberately avoids a direct contrast between the Spirit of God and the spirit of antichrist, because John does not view them as equal and opposing spirits. But the NIV's reading makes good sense in the context of the passage, which is in fact contrasting the two spirits.

is personal, for it is a person's commitment to Jesus Christ. In this light, the prophets who apparently deny *that Jesus Christ has come in the flesh* manifest *the spirit of the antichrist,* because they deny Jesus. They have left the fellowship he calls together; they have ignored his atoning death; they failed to preserve the Johannine teaching about him; and they have violated his commandments. In short, they have failed to align themselves with him. In John's dualistically oriented world view, such a failure can be stated in its harshest terms as the opposition of the end time, expected in the antichrist (v. 3; 2:18-19). The defectors have the spirit of antichrist, a spirit opposed to the Spirit of God because it ranges itself against the Son of God, Jesus Christ, and what he calls people to be and do (3:23).

Spirit-inspired Victory (4:4) All who deny Jesus are called *the world* (4:3-5). They belong to that sphere of existence opposed to or ignorant of God's spirit and ways (2:15-17). By way of reassurance, the Elder contrasts his readers with the secessionists: they are of the world, but *you, dear children, are from God.* They can be sure of their relationship with God because they *have overcome them,* the false prophets (4:1). The word *overcome (nikaō)* implies a conflict in which one party emerges victorious (compare 1 Jn 2:13-14; 5:4-5; Jn 16:33). The victorious party is the Johannine Christians, and their victory is their faithfulness to Jesus Christ. Victory in this instance is virtually equivalent to resisting false teaching and to holding to the truth.

Even though the Elder writes that *you . . . have overcome,* it is clear that the victory won by believers is neither the product of their own effort nor the result of their own merits. Victory comes from God, who is *greater than the one who is in the world,* the "prince of this world" (Jn 12:31; 14:30; 16:11), also known in Johannine thought as the evil one (2:13-14). The assertions about victory in verse 4 have several implications: First, the conflict between the Johannine community and the dissidents is but a reflection of a greater struggle between truth and error, between the Spirit of truth and the spirit of antichrist. But John does not see this struggle played out in a world far above and beyond human

---

4:4 The phrase *the one who is in you* uses a masculine definite article. This suggests that the author is thinking of God (a masculine noun in Greek; Marshall 1978:208 n. 16; Houlden

beings. Hence this is also a human struggle, a conflict between the commitments of one group of people with those of another group. Our faith is itself our victory (5:4). Moreover, those who *have overcome* have done so by remaining faithful to the God who overcomes all evil. The Johannine Christians can test their allegiance and reassure themselves of their status as children of God by their steadfastness. Above all, these words are designed to bring assurance to believers.

Spirit-inspired Response (4:5-6) Here the Elder adduces a second way by which one may *test the spirits,* by evaluating the response that the speaker receives. Those who are *from the world* will be heard and accepted by others who likewise dwell within the sphere of the world. But those who are from God are heard by those who know God. These verses echo the sentiments of John 15:18-23, that the response of the world to Jesus' disciples mirrors its response to Jesus and, in the final analysis, to God. Reversing this chain of response, John can also say that those who have responded to God positively also respond to Jesus and to his disciples by listening to them. Listening means far more than simply giving them a hearing; it implies agreement with what is heard. After all, Jesus promised his followers the Spirit of truth who would "teach [them] all things" (14:26) and "guide [them] into all truth" (16:13). The Spirit inspires both teaching and understanding of the truth. Similarly, Paul expects that the Holy Spirit inspires those who speak in tongues and those who interpret them, and that the Spirit inspires prophets and those who discern the truth of prophecy (1 Cor 2:11; 12:7-11, 29-31; 14:28-33).

Looking back over the entire section (4:1-6), the Elder ends the section by writing, *this is how we recognize the Spirit of truth and the spirit of falsehood.* He has offered two explicit "tests": the content of christological confession and the reception that the message receives. Both confession and response are inspired by the Spirit who inspires and guards the truth of the word of life.

It might now seem that we have a definitive "field guide" to discerning the spirits. We are given two clear tests by which we may be able to tell

---

1973:110), not the Spirit (a neuter noun; Brown 1982:498; Bruce 1970:106; Stott 1988:160).

truth from error, divine inspiration from delusion and deception. And not only do we have the tests, we have an exhortation to put them to use. How then are we to go about testing the Spirits? In what circumstances is such testing important and even necessary? If "testing the Spirits" implies rejecting what is false, are we to reject both the teaching and the teacher? We may suggest three guidelines as to how we can *test the Spirits* with discernment, that is, with wisdom, care and humility.

1. We are called on as a *corporate community* to *test the spirits.* The *spirits* that are in view are the teachings and practices that threaten the church's mission and teaching. In John's view, whatever denies the centrality of Christ and his work in mediating knowledge of God would be detrimental to the health of the church and would compromise its mission. Together with other faithful members of the community, we are called on to wrestle with the difficult and complex issue of discerning how we are to understand and formulate the word of life so that it is heard as life-giving for people today.

2. It is also crucial to remember *what* we are called on to test. We are not called to test every single belief and practice of every individual who claims to be a Christian. In context, 1 John is dealing with the beliefs that the Christian community ought to hold in order to maintain its continuity with the affirmations of the apostles and eyewitnesses. The Elder is arguing for what the church must believe and guard in order to interpret faithfully the revelation of God in Jesus Christ. Therefore, it follows that those in positions of authority and leadership have the charge to interpret and teach God's truth responsibly. We can require of them a standard of theological understanding and faithfulness that we might not ask of all church members. On the other hand, that does not mean that the church may simply allow its members to believe and do whatever they want. It is the church's responsibility to nurture and nourish its members, to teach, encourage, exhort and reprove them, to bring them into conformity with what it understands to be the truth. "Discerning the spirits" is not simply an end in itself.

3. We are called on to discern what is *central* to Christian faith and doctrine. Within the life of the church, some issues are more central than others, and few if any are more central than Christology (the doctrine of Christ) and soteriology (how we receive salvation). The confession

of "Jesus Christ Incarnate" provides a test for how we are to understand Jesus. It would not be acceptable for a church to say that it does not matter how we understand Jesus, or that we may abandon John's affirmation that in Jesus we encounter God's revelatory word and so come to salvation in knowing God. But we must remember that the epistle does not give us a detailed explanation of exactly what "Jesus Christ Incarnate" means, nor does it address such issues as the manner of the Incarnation, the relationship of the "two natures" of Jesus and so on. We must be careful, then, on insisting that others believe exactly as we do when the Scriptures are silent or difficult to interpret with certainty. Typically this is where disagreements arise. There is nothing wrong with the guide, but those who use it are not always skilled in doing so. Even an infallible guide can be misused, for it is always used by fallible people.

In sum, two extremes are to be avoided. On the one hand, we ought not to rush to judgment on others. But, on the other hand, the church cannot avoid its task to teach and nurture people in the Christian faith. And to do so responsibly it must in every age and generation *test the spirits,* that is, approve and cherish that which is true because it comes from God's own Spirit of truth.

Let Us Love One Another (4:7-12)   One of the best-known works of Western art is surely that section of the ceiling of the Sistine Chapel which depicts God reaching down to touch Adam's fingertip and give him life. So well known is this portion of Michelangelo's monumental work that it appears not merely in art histories and coffee-table display books, but is also used and caricatured in advertising and political cartoons. Only the most jaded of tourists can fail to marvel when gazing up at the mural, so laboriously and painstakingly painted, so powerful in its depiction of the life-giving power of God. We stop, study, appraise and admire. What a masterpiece! What an artist!

In this section of the epistle, John writes, *This is how God showed his love among us: He sent his one and only Son into the world* (v. 9). We might be tempted to exclaim, What a masterpiece! What an artist! But "The Sending of the Son" is not simply the title of a painting that we study, admire and appreciate. Michelangelo's painting has power not just because of its artistic merits, but because we can virtually feel the life that flows from God's hand to Adam. Even so, John writes not just that *God showed his love among us* but that he did so by sending the Son into the world *that we might live through him.*

God's life-giving love, then, is the theme of this passage. As John develops this theme, he makes three important points: God is the *source* of all love (4:7-8); God *models* what genuine love is (4:9-10); and God *commands* us to love each other (4:11-12). We move from the assertion that God *is* love to the command that we are to love each other. Indeed, the whole point of the passage is to trace the relationship between God's love and human love, and to show how human love flows from God's own love.

The Source of Love (4:7-8) In exploring the relationship between God's love for us and our love for each other, the Elder makes two statements: *love comes from God* (v. 7), and *God is love* (v. 8). The second statement is more far-reaching than the first. To comprehend the sweeping character of the statement *God is love,* substitute the name of anyone you know—your mother, pastor, friend, a well-known Christian or hero of the faith or even yourself—for "God." Few are the people we would describe simply with the word *love.* Mom may be the most loving person you have known. She may have shown you what mature, self-giving, genuine love is like. But no matter how full, rich and steadfast her love, the statement "Mom is loving," can never be changed into "Mom is love." For love does not characterize her as it characterizes God.

Because God is love, *love comes from God.* God is the source of love. Like the electricity running through electrical wires, love comes from God to us, then flows through us to others in the community. When John exhorts his readers, *let us love one another,* he is encouraging them to allow God's love to flow through them. For because *God is love,* love

---

Notes: 4:7 In the statement *Everyone who loves has been born of God,* the object of the verb *love* is not stated. Brown (1982:514) and Bultmann (1973:65-66) assume that the Elder is speaking of love for others; Schnackenburg (1963:228-29), Smalley (1984:234) and Stott (1988:163) argue that love of both God and neighbor is in view. The exhortation *let us love one another* (compare v. 11) and the statement *if we love each other, God lives in us* (v. 12) support the view that here *love* is love for other Christians.

The phrases *everyone who (pas* plus the definite article) and *whoever* (v. 8) do not mean "anyone at all," but "everyone" viewed as two distinct groups: those in the church and those

must characterize those who claim to be *born of God* or to *know God* (v. 7; 3:10, 14; 4:20-21). Those who claim to be doing the will of God and reflecting God's activity in the world will be known by the love they manifest for God and for each other. This was what Jesus told his disciples (Jn 13:35).

It is typical of the Elder that, having stated his case in positive terms, he then states it negatively: *Whoever does not love, does not know God.* Where there is a lack of love for fellow Christians, there is neither love for nor knowledge of God. As John Stott puts it, claiming to know God while failing to love others is like claiming to have intimate knowledge of a foreigner while remaining ignorant of his or her native tongue (1988:114). In their historical context, the statements about those who do not love are probably directed to the secessionists. Although these people undoubtedly claimed to know God, the Elder deems such a claim impossible: for how can one who lacks love for God's children be said to know the God who is love? Their lack of love shows that the dissidents are not in touch with the source of love (4:8, 16), they do not imitate the model of love given to them in the cross (3:16; 4:10) and they have disobeyed the command of Jesus (2:7; 4:21; Jn 13:34-35; 15:12, 17). In short, their claim to know God is hollow.

The Model of Love (4:9-10) Also typical of 1 John, the discussion does not remain on the abstract level. Following the general statement *love comes from God,* the epistle here begins to speak of the specific manifestation of that love in the sending of the only Son. God's love is a *model* for how and why we are to love each other. The Elder emphasizes the visible manifestation of love (v. 9); its active and redeeming character (vv. 9-10); and its ultimate definition in terms of God's action rather than our own (v. 10). We may look briefly at these three items.

First, just as God's love was manifested in the sending of the Son, so

---

who have departed. The repeated use of *everyone who* underscores John's dualistic world view; see Brown (1982:353, 514).

4:9 The prepositional phrase *among us (en hēmin)* can be taken with the verb *showed* or with the noun *love.* Although some commentators (Culpepper 1985:88; Kysar 1986:96; TEV) take the phrase as modifying *love,* the majority take it as modifying *showed.* In either case, the meaning of the preposition *en* is disputed. It is construed either as a *dative,* meaning "to us" or "for us," thus giving the translation "God's love was manifested to us";

John expects that we will demonstrate love in action to others (compare 3:16-18). Christians will live out their love in kindness, generosity and service to others. But, second, the Elder's argument moves quickly beyond the example that God's love provides for us to an examination of its active and redeeming character (vv. 9-10). God has loved us in a way that has given us life. The atoning death of Jesus provides the means by which believers come into a life-giving realm where love is received and expressed (Jn 3:16). We do not simply gaze at the painting on the wall; we are touched by the hand of God and given life-giving love. And, third, because life and love come from God, it is God's activity and not our own behavior and efforts that defines the essence of love.

The Command to Love (4:11-12) Because God's children have experienced such love, the command that comes to them to love each other is not the "ought" of external compulsion but the "ought" of internal constraint (Bruce 1970:109). On its own, the commandment cannot provide the incentive or the power to fulfill it, and this might foster either discouragement or indifference. But those who are in touch with the very source of love, who have been shown what love is and who are the recipients of a great and healing love, can receive the commandment with hope and joy. For they are not commanded to do something that is alien to their experience or beyond their ability to learn and to do.

So strong is John's confidence that the Christian community will fulfill this command that he writes that mutual Christian love manifests the presence and action of the invisible God (v. 12; Smalley 1984:246). When he writes *no one has ever seen God,* he calls to mind the same statement in the Gospel of John (1:18). In both cases, he is not trying to tell us what God is like but how God is known. And God is known not only in the revelation that comes to us in Jesus (Jn 1:18) but also by the manifestation of our love for each other (1 Jn 4:12). The love of

---

or as showing the *locale* of the revelation of love. In the latter case, there are again several options: "within" or "in" us, explaining the personal nature of God's love for us (Culpepper 1985:88); "among us," with reference to the church (Schnackenburg 1963:229 n. 4) or perhaps the church and the world (Smalley 1984:240-41). Elsewhere in John and 1 John one finds the ideas of God's love for the world (Jn 3:16), of God's special self-manifestation among and love for believers (Jn 1:14; 1 Jn 1:1-3; 3:1-3, 16), and of God's indwelling love

believers makes evident and concrete the activity of God among them. In fact, when the Elder writes that this is how *[God's] love is made complete,* he means that it reaches its intended goal when it flows from God, through us, to our fellow believers. The love with which God loved us must in turn be extended to the fellowship of believers.

In short, God not only gives us the command to love but has also modeled for us what true love is, just as Jesus modeled love for his disciples when he washed their feet before his death (Jn 13:1-17). Love that does not express itself concretely and in service to others is not love (1 Jn 3:16-18). But even more, God also empowers us to love. By confession of the Son whom God has sent, we are born of God and come to know God, who is love (v. 7); we are given life (v. 9); our sins are forgiven (v. 10). We come into the realm of life and love, in which we are given life and are empowered to extend the same kind of life-giving love to others. We come to know the source of love.

Abiding in Faith and Love (4:13—5:5) What is love? is a question asked by theologians, philosophers and ethicists; by romantic poets and adolescents; by betrayed spouses and abandoned children; by the hopeful and the hopeless; by the dreamy-eyed and the cynical. Answers to the question are many. And, sadly enough, many of the answers betray a hard-edged cynicism. The familiar folk song "Lemon Tree" has a father giving his son this advice: "Don't put your faith in love, my boy. . . . I fear you'll find that love is like the lovely lemon tree . . . very pretty, and the lemon flower is sweet, but the fruit of the poor lemon is impossible to eat." In short, dream about love, sing about it, write about it—but avoid it, for it does not bring hope and joy, only hopelessness and bitterness.

The author of 1 John has a different view of the matter. Simply and boldly he writes, *God is love.* Inadvertently this often gets turned around

---

(3:17). Both the love of God *for* as well as indwelling *in* believers is in view in verse 9 (compare v. 10).

The adjective *only* translates the Greek *monogenē,* and means "one of a kind, singular." The alternate reading "only begotten" comes from Jerome's translation of the New Testament into Latin. Neither the Gospel nor the epistles of John speak of the Son as "begotten" of God as believers are.

to read "love is God." If love is God, then it is what we live for, what we serve, the ultimate standard of all. Augustine wrote that, prior to his conversion, "I loved not yet, yet I loved to love. . . . I sought what I might love, in love with loving" (*Confessions* 3.1). Love itself was what was sought, cherished, hoped for. Love is, as one pop song of the sixties had it, "all you need."

But John does not write "love is God," that love is the final and supreme good. He writes, *God is love*. If we want to know what love is, then we must let God define it. As Frederick Buechner comments, "To say that love is God is romantic idealism. To say that God is love is either the last straw or the ultimate truth" (1973:54). For John, it is indeed the ultimate truth. God is not hate, anger, bitterness or deceit, but love. Love does not describe the fullness of God, but God defines the fullness of love. In this section of the epistle (4:13—5:5), we are shown that God is the *standard* of love (4:13-16); the one who *encourages* us in love (4:17-18); the *source* of love (4:19-20); and the one who *commands* us to love (4:21—5:5).

God Is the Standard of Love (4:13-16) When we say that God is the "standard" for love, we mean that God's actions reveal to us what love is and how it manifests itself. Earlier John had argued that there is a concrete manifestation of God's presence and activity in the Christian community in the love of Christians for each other (4:7-12). Now he asserts that God's love for us is manifested in sending Jesus as the Savior of the world (vv. 15-16). If we have never seen God (vv. 12, 20), we have seen that the Son has been sent for our salvation. The "seeing" referred to here is the sight of faith (Barker 1981:345; Smalley 1984:252; compare Jn 9:37-41). What the eyewitnesses saw (1 Jn 1:1-4) and what all subsequent believers have experienced in Jesus by faith was God's act of salvation for the world. Some physically saw Jesus; but perceiving that Jesus is the life of the world is not limited to eyewitnesses. As an African

Notes: 4:14 Although some commentators (Schnackenburg 1963:242; Stott 1988:169) take the *we* of verse 13 as referring primarily to the eyewitnesses of Jesus' ministry, others take *have seen* in a figurative sense, so that *we* refers more broadly either to all Johannine believers or to all Christians (Brown 1982:523). Still others see the *we* as deliberately inclusive, referring to both eyewitnesses and later generations of disciples (Bruce 1970:110-11; Culpepper 1985:90; Dodd 1946:115; Marshall 1978:220 n. 5). The emphasis falls not on what the eyewitnesses saw, but rather on the assurance that the community has because of the reality that they have experienced and in which they believe. Compare John 4:42, where

proverb has it, "God has no grandchildren." All believers come to God on the same footing as those who heard and saw and followed Jesus.

The confession of Jesus as the Son of God and Savior of the world encapsulates the Johannine understanding of Jesus. First, Jesus is the *Son of God.* Because Jesus is the Son, he stands in a unique relationship with God; therefore, he mediates salvation (v. 14), the indwelling of God with us (v. 15) and the love of God (v. 16). Second, Jesus is *Savior.* His life and death mediate salvation or fellowship with God (1:3; 4:2; compare Jn 17:3). Jesus makes God known and takes away sin (2:2; 3:5, 8; 4:10) so that we may indeed have fellowship with God. Third, Jesus is the Savior *of the world.* This affirmation summarizes the universal scope of Jesus' work: no one, even the one hostile to God, stands outside the scope of God's love. Salvation is appropriated by the person who *acknowledges that Jesus is the Son of God.*

All that Jesus is and does testifies to and manifests God's love. Those who confess Jesus as Son of God and Savior *know and rely on the love God has for us. Rely on* suggests the trustworthy nature of that in which we put our trust. Christians can count on the steadfastness of God's love, because they have experienced it in God's faithfulness to them. They can rely on God. The cynical songwriter who counseled, "Don't put your faith in love" really meant "don't put your faith in people." But John writes that we can trust God's love, because we can trust God. The evidence of God's steadfast love is the sending of the Son (1 Jn 3:16; 4:10; Jn 3:16). It is impossible to confess the Son without at the same time understanding him to be the incomparable manifestation of God's love.

So in verse 16 the Elder moves easily into a reassertion of his earlier thesis that *God is love,* a statement that is difficult to improve upon, explain or paraphrase. We can say that God's nature is love, that God's actions are loving, that God repeatedly demonstrates love for us and

---

the Samaritans say, "We have *heard* for ourselves, and we know that this man really is the Savior of the world." There is no substantive distinction between "seeing" and "hearing" this truth.

4:16 The NIV translates the prepositional phrase *en hēmin* as *for us;* the same phrase is translated *among us* in 4:9. Brown (1982:525), Culpepper (1985:91), Kysar (1986:100), Marshall (1978:221) and Smalley (1984:255) prefer the reading "in us" at 4:16, emphasizing the indwelling love of God. The point of the statement is the affirmation of the experience

others, that God loved even a hostile world and that God sent Jesus to make all of this known to us. That God's love provides the standard for love means that authentic love is steadfast and constant, that it is directed toward others with life-giving healing, that it seeks out its enemies for good and that it is known pre-eminently in the cross. Human love derives its character and shape from the standard of divine love.

As noted above, we must not turn the affirmation *God is love* around to read "love is God." The second part of verse 16 lends itself to such a misreading when it says *whoever lives in love lives in God.* But the Elder can write *whoever lives in love lives in God* only because he has first written *God is love.* In other words, he assumes that those who love live in God—but only because he assumes that those who live in God necessarily love. Love comes from God who is love; hence, those who live in love show that they live in God. Love for others and living in relationship with God are inseparable. The dissidents who claim to live in God, although they do not love the children of God, live neither in love nor in God.

God Encourages Us in Love (4:17-18) The relationship of divine and human love is further developed here. God makes our love *complete* and so gives us confidence. As noted above in the comments on verse 12, love that is *complete* is love that reaches its goal by being bestowed upon our brother or sister. To put it another way, the shape of perfect love is triangular: love comes as a gift from God that enables us to love each other and so return to God the gift that is given to us. In the words of C. H. Dodd, "The energy of love discharges itself along lines which form a triangle, whose points are God, self, and neighbour." Where any one leg of the triangle is missing, love remains incomplete and immature.

---

of God's love, personally and communally, and this interpretation holds no matter which translation is adopted.

Barker (1981:345), Grayston (1984:129), Marshall (1978:221), Smalley (1984:255) and Stott (1988:170-71) are among those who read verse 16 as one complete thought, rather than dividing it into two parts with the NIV. The statement *God is love* flows from and provides the rationale for the previous statement *we rely on the love God has for us.*

4:17 The original NIV did not translate the Greek *en toutō* at this point. Here *en toutō* ("this is how") refers to the preceding thought (so Brown 1982:527; Culpepper 1985:92; Marshall 1978:223 n. 17; Smalley 1984:257). These verses are closely connected and ought to be read as follows: "Whoever lives in love lives in God, and God in him. This is how love is made complete among us . . ." The later edition of the NIV reads *In this way, love*

But where the triangle is whole, love is complete. As a result, we *have confidence on the day of judgment* because our love signals to us that we already enjoy fellowship with God. And those who share fellowship with God in the present need not fear that they shall be judged unfavorably in the future. God will not take away from them the salvation and love that has already been granted to them in the Son. They need have no fear of punishment.

The Elder further underscores the point when he writes, *in this world we are like him.* Here is an analogy between the children of God and the Son of God at the point of fellowship with God (compare Jn 17:21-23). As the Son has free access to and confidence with God (2:1), so too does the believer have a boldness with God (2:28; 3:19-22; 4:18; 5:14). And since boldness and fear are opposites of each other, the author writes that in love—the hallmark of our relationship to God and of Jesus' relationship to God—there is only confidence: not fear. As Barclay puts it, "When love comes, fear goes" (1976:98).

And so John writes, *There is no fear in love. But perfect love drives out fear.* As the context shows, *fear* means fear of punishment by God when one comes to the judgment. Those who live in God do not need to fear God's judgment. But the statement ought not to be turned around to mean that any anxieties or fears are evidence that we are imperfect in love. Confidence and fear are opposites, and the Elder believes that because Christians have confidence before God they need not be frightened of God's judgment. Fear of being condemned has been driven out from them by the perfect love of God.

Nonetheless, many Christians are tortured by feelings of worthlessness, self-doubt and inadequacy, that they are not good enough for God,

---

is made complete . . .

There is a catalog of interpretations of the phrase *because in this world we are like him* in Brown (1982:529). It has been suggested that we are like Christ in his incarnate, human life, in his love and in his moral life. Most recent commentators argue that it refers to relationship with God (so Barker 1981:346; Brown 1982:529; Culpepper 1985:94; Marshall 1978:223; Smalley 1984:259; Stott 1988:171-72). Houlden (1973:119) suggests that it refers to Christ's perfect confidence. The ideas of confidence and indwelling are closely related, here and throughout 1 John. Elsewhere in the epistle, Jesus is our advocate with God (2:2); on that model, believers are encouraged to approach God with confidence (3:19-22; 5:14). But such confidence and boldness in making requests are available only to those who are children of God (3:2), who share that intimate relationship of mutual indwelling.

that somehow by trying harder they really can make God love them more. A young Christian counselor once told me of working with a woman who had great difficulty accepting God's unconditional love for her. His well-meaning but misguided strategy was to exhort her, "You just have to believe it." But we cannot badger others into accepting God's love. Although we can preach and teach about it, and try to model it in our life and community, each of us must ultimately open up with vulnerability and humility to acknowledge our unworthiness and yet also to accept our own worth, which is sometimes the more difficult. In confessing our sin before God, we accept our *unworthiness—not* worthlessness! In that moment of vulnerability we discover that God is "faithful and just" and, through Jesus Christ, graciously covers the sinner with love and forgiveness. We know that although we have been found out, we have also been found. We come to accept that God sent the Son into the world because he deemed us *worthy* to be loved and forgiven, we who are created in the divine image and destined to become fully restored to it when "we shall be like him, for we shall see him as he is" (3:2).

To know that we are forgiven for our sin, loved in our weakness, saved by his mercy, destined for fellowship with God, all because we are supremely valued by God—that is to know the perfect love that drives fear away. It is not because of what we have done that we can have such confidence before God, but because of what God has done for us.

God Is the Source of Love (4:19-20) The Elder has not yet finished with his reflections on love. The statement *We love because he first loved us* summarizes the relationship of human and divine love, and especially the previous verses (vv. 7-18). Quite simply, the Elder states that God's love for us has empowered us to love both other human beings and God. Yet God does not give us some power or ability apart from his own presence that motivates us to love. God loves us, and it is the very love of God that empowers us to love. The gift cannot be

---

4:21 It is not clear whether the command to love is understood to come from God or from Jesus. Barker (1981:347), Houlden (1973:120 n. 2), Smith (1991:116) and Stott (1988:273-74) and the NEB and TEV assume that verse 21 means Jesus; others, that it means God (Marshall 1978:225 n. 28, 226; Schnackenburg 1963:250); and still others that it refers to God's command as expressed in the teaching of Jesus (Dodd 1946:123; Grayston 1984:132, and n. 2; Smalley 1984:265). Ultimately the command to love is God's own

separated from the Giver. For love is enabling power, and those who have known themselves loved by God are empowered to love. Love is a life-giving force, an invigorating gift that flows from God into human beings with vitality and energy. Love—being loved and knowing that one is loved—empowers us to love.

And so if God's love empowers us to love, no one can claim to love God while hating a fellow Christian (4:20). Often the words *anyone who does not love his brother, whom he has seen, cannot love God, whom he has not seen* are taken to mean that it is much *harder* to love an invisible God than it is to love a brother or sister whom one can see. But John does not say that love for God is more difficult than love for others. Rather, love for God without love for others is simply impossible to imagine, since *God is love.* As Stott comments, "This 'cannot' expresses not so much the person's incapacity to love God, as the proof that he does not" (1988:173; compare Dodd 1946:123-24; Marshall 1978:225-26; Smalley 1984:264).

God Commands Us to Love (4:21—5:5) And, finally, John tells us that God commands us to love. Whether we are speaking of love of God or love of others, love epitomizes the divine will for human beings, since God is love. All those who are children of God, who confess Jesus as the Christ, are to love each other. Two parallel statements in 5:1 both begin, *everyone who . . .* One points to the importance of faith in Jesus, the other to the importance of loving each other. These are not two separate commands that one must keep in order to become a child of God; rather, they are two expressions of what the child of God does. Faith and love are each expressions of the work of God in a person's life. Each is centered in the person of Jesus Christ: our faith is in Jesus as the Messiah of God, who provides the fundamental manifestation of God's love for us.

The Greek makes the connection between loving God and loving each other clear in a rather elaborate play on words (somewhat obscured by

command; but the command was given to us by Jesus, and Jesus' life and teaching were always in conformity with God's will.

5:1 The NIV mixes its metaphors when it uses both *born of God* and the father/child relationship. Compare the RSV, which endeavors to keep the parallelism in idiomatic English: "Every one who believes that Jesus is the Christ is a *child* of God, and every one who loves the *parent* loves the *child*."

the NIV). *Born of God, father,* and *child* all have roots in the same Greek verb *(gennaō).* A literal but wooden translation would read, "Everyone who believes that Jesus is the Messiah has been begotten of God, and the one who loves the one who begets, loves the one who is begotten of him." The Elder emphasizes the inevitability and necessity of loving both the child and the parent, since the one is intimately related to the other. "Begetting" obviously points to the relationship of the parent and child, but it also establishes an affinity and an affection between the children who are begotten (Stott 1988:175).

Love for the children of God is one criterion by which we test the veracity of the claim to know and to love God, and this has been stated regularly in the epistle (3:17; 4:12, 20-21; 5:1). But verse 2 turns this thought around by stating that we can be assured that we love the children of God if we love God. This is by far the harder idea, since, as the Elder has already acknowledged, *no one has ever seen God.* How, then, can love for God provide the evidence that we love others?

One helpful clue is offered immediately: we know that we love God *by carrying out [God's] commands.* In fact in verse 3 we have virtually a definition of love for God: it is *to obey [God's] commands.* Certainly the commands in question would include the command to love (4:21), as well as the command to "believe in the name of his Son, Jesus Christ" (3:23). The somewhat unusual usage of the plural *commands* suggests again that 5:1 speaks of two things—believing and loving—that simultaneously characterize believers and that manifest that one knows and loves God.

But does obeying the commands completely exhaust the meaning of "love of God"? Probably they are not equivalent. Rather John means that love of God will express itself in obedience to God's commands. Nev-

---

5:2 Marshall (1978:227) suggests that we read the first part of verse 2 as a virtual statement of obligation: "This is how we know that we *should love* the children of God." The statement refers to 5:1, where it was asserted that children love the [other] children of their parent. But then the subordinate statements in the rest of verse 2 are left dangling. In this case *this is how we know* refers forward (see Brown 1982:537-38).

5:3 The reason that the commands are not *burdensome* is drawn either from the nature of the commands themselves ("they are not beyond our ability to keep"; Marshall 1978:228; Stott 1988:176; Grayston 1984:133 thinks that this refers to the small number of commands that are given); or from the power God gives us to keep them (Barker 1981:349; Brown

ertheless, the emphasis on living out one's commitment to God by obedience rescues the concept of loving God from the purely private realm. Those who love God do what pleases God, just as children want to please their parents. Since the Elder views the dissidents as failing to do what pleases God, he also finds their claim to love God invalid.

To speak of doing what pleases God can lead some people to imagine that it is by doing *enough* of what pleases God that we somehow gain approval or favor in God's eyes. But pleasing God and keeping God's commands cannot be measured statistically. Pleasing God is the response to God's love in our lives. Thus the commands of God *are not burdensome.* God's commands are not demands extraneous to us, imposed upon us, to which we must measure up. In fact, the Elder seems to deny that fulfilling the commands is possible by human power or initiative when he writes that we love because of God's prior love (4:19) and confess Jesus by inspiration of the Spirit (4:2).

To put it another way, we fulfill the commands because the one born of God *has overcome the world.* This statement of God's victory in us provides the real basis for why the commands are not burdensome. The word translated "overcome" *(nikaō)* has the same root as the word "victory" *(nikē).* "Overcoming" means gaining the victory in a contest. In 1 John the victory of believers has different manifestations (2:13-14; 4:4). But it is in essence *one* victory—namely, a victory over the powers that oppose God and in overt and subtle ways have sought to turn them from God. Those born of God have resisted the forces that try to hold them captive in the world by persuading them to abandon their true faith in Christ and join the realm of the unbelievers. But the Johannine Christians have stood firm. They *have* faith in God, and they *hold* to faith in God. The Elder stresses the present reality of their victory; he does not

---

1982:541; Bruce 1970:117; Culpepper 1985:100; Dodd 1946:126; Houlden 1973:124; Smalley 1984:269). Some commentators think that both ideas are in view (Marshall 1978:228; Stott 1988:176). The statements that God's love empowers our love (4:19) and God's Spirit inspires our confession (4:1, 6, 13-15) suggest that God's power enables people to keep the commands God gives (3:23).

5:4 *Everyone born of God* in the NIV renders a Greek neuter plural, "all that is born of God." The neuter plural refers to the group in its collective aspect: "all those begotten by God inasmuch as they are begotten." Those who are begotten by God have overcome the world, by virtue of their being begotten.

write that believers *can* overcome or that they *will* overcome, but that they have that victory now.

"Victorious faith" in this context means continuing steadfastly in their faith that Jesus is the Son of God and that through his mediation they have passed from death to life, they have overcome the world (3:13-14), they continue to receive life (2:1-2; 5:13) and they are kept safe from the evil one (5:18). Faith is not the means to the goal of victory, nor something that enables us to gain victory: faith *is* the victory, and not because of what faith is in itself but because it is directed to the Son, through whom God wins the victory for us (5:6-12).

To have such faith is to have the kind of trust in God that children have in their parents. And they have such trust because of their experience of the faithfulness and love of their parents for them. So the call for faith and the call for love are really one. Although the Elder repeatedly emphasizes the importance of Christian love for each other, that obligation is not arbitrarily imposed. Rather the call to love is derived from the very nature of God, who is love, and who loves us and encourages, commands and empowers us to love. Indeed, God's saving work is at heart a work of love, for it brings us into a household of filial and familial relationships, in which Jesus is the foundation and love the mortar. We are called to trust in the God who is love. For John, *God is love* is not romantic idealism or the last straw: it is the ultimate truth.

Testimony to the Son (5:6-12)   To what source of authority ought today's Christians turn in trying to settle disputed matters of the faith? To the guidance of the Holy Spirit? The confessions of the church? Events of history? The personal testimony of believers? The Scriptures? Some Christians would be tempted, perhaps, to say immediately "to Scrip-

---

Notes: 5:6 The three most common interpretations of *came by water and blood* are as follows: (1) The water and blood refer to the sacraments of baptism and the Lord's Supper. (2) The water and blood refer to Jesus' baptism and crucifixion. Commentators who hold this view stress that *water and blood* covers Jesus' incarnate life and earthly career from beginning to end, showing either his genuine Incarnation and full humanity, or the saving significance of his entire life (Bruce 1970:118-19; Houlden 1973:127; Marshall 1978:232-33; Smalley 1984:278-79; Stott 1988:180-81). (3) The water and blood refer to Jesus' death, and to the event associated with it in the Gospel of John (Brown 1982:574; Grayston 1984:136-38; Kysar 1986:107-8; Smith 1991:123-24). One of the main arguments against this third view

ture"—and only to Scripture. Others would choose another of the options above, or perhaps some combination of them, always granting Scripture pride of place. In this regard 1 John is especially instructive, for in settling the christological debate in its community it never appeals to the Old Testament, and it cannot appeal to the New Testament, which did not yet exist as a collection of documents. But the present passage, in trying to underscore the importance of confession of Jesus, does appeal to the guidance of the Spirit, to a christological formula preserved by the community, to the word of reliable individuals and to the events of history. Here, then, we learn how the author sees a historical event, the inspiration of the Spirit and the teaching of the church all joining together in bearing a common witness to the truth.

The topic of discussion in 5:6-12 is appropriate confession about Jesus (compare 4:2). Here the desired confession is that Jesus Christ is the one *who came by water and blood.* But exactly what it means to say that Jesus *came by water and blood* remains as much a matter of debate today as it probably was in John's own time!

The "Blood and Water" Witness to Jesus Christ (5:6) To understand the point being made by the use of this phrase, it will be helpful to examine the use of "water" and "blood" in the Gospel and the epistles of John. While *water* is mentioned in the epistles only here, several significant references to it are found in the Gospel. The Baptist baptizes with water (1:26, 31, 33), as does Jesus (3:22; 4:1-2), and the water symbolizes cleansing. Jesus changes water set aside for the Jewish rites of purification to wine (2:1-12). He speaks of the necessity to be born of "water and the Spirit" (3:5, 8), where "water and Spirit" probably connotes one idea, namely, cleansing by the Holy Spirit (compare Ezek 36:25-27). Thus water also symbolizes the gift of the Spirit (4:13-14; 7:37-

---

has traditionally been that the statement *not . . . by water only, but by water and blood* demands that *water* and *blood* must refer to two separate comings, both of which the author affirms. However, Brown (1982:574) rightly questions that assertion. The Elder is not affirming two separate comings—one by water and another by blood. Rather he is denying the secessionists' claim that he came by water by asserting that he came by water *and* blood. This is essentially one event. But because in Johannine tradition (Jn 6:51-58; 1 Jn 1:7) "blood," taken by itself, refers to the saving death of Jesus and the necessity of forgiveness, John repeats that part of the statement only.

39) given by the risen Jesus. Together these references stress the idea of purifying, and particularly the purifying effected by the Spirit of God.

Except for the passage under consideration, *blood* appears in the epistles only in 1 John 1:7, where it is said that "the blood of Jesus purifies us from every sin." In the Gospel "blood" stands for Jesus' self-sacrifice in death (6:51-58), without which there is no eternal life. Right relationship with God, whether described in terms of being purified or having eternal life, depends upon the death of Jesus.

One passage in the Gospel of John does bring together the images of water and blood. When the soldiers pierce Jesus' side at the crucifixion, it is said that "blood and water" flowed from it (19:34). This is understood as evidence that Jesus had indeed died, a necessary corroboration since the soldiers had not expected to find him already dead. It is likely that this story has symbolic importance as well. In light of the imagery of water and blood in the Gospel, the water and blood from Jesus' side signify that his death releases the gift of the Spirit (water) and purification from sin (blood), which together confer eternal life. As Barrett aptly phrases it, John intends us to see in this event that "the real death of Jesus was the real life of men" (1978:557).

How then does this fit with 1 John? While *water* does not appear elsewhere in 1 John, a reference to the *blood* of Jesus appears as part of a refutation of the dissidents' claims that they are without sin and without need for the cleansing understood to come through Jesus' blood (1:7). Similarly, here the "coming by blood" may be a reference to Jesus' "cleansing blood," that is, to his death that purifies believers from sin. If 1 John 5:6 is referring to the incident at Jesus' crucifixion, when water and blood came out from his side, then the confession that Jesus came by water and blood points to his death as the culmination of his saving mission. Salvation came with Jesus, and it was not accomplished without his death. Indeed, Jesus himself speaks the words that guide our interpretation when he says from the cross, "It is finished" (Jn 19:30): his saving mission is brought to its fulfillment in his death. After his death, Jesus also gave the Spirit, and through the Spirit we are born anew so that we are children of God (Jn 3:3, 5). But the giving of the Spirit was contingent upon and subsequent to Jesus' death on the cross (Jn 14:26; 15:26; 16:7).

The epistle has changed the order of the Gospel's phrase "blood and water" to *water and blood* in order to emphasize the blood, as the next part of the verse shows: not *by water only, but by water and blood.* Although both water and blood came forth from Jesus' side, it is Jesus' atoning sacrifice for sin that needs underscoring. We recall that the secessionists may have been claiming that the Spirit conferred upon them the status of children of God, and by virtue of that status they had no sin and needed no further cleansing (see 1:8-10). John reminds his readers of the continued centrality of Jesus' death. Not only does it continue to provide needed atonement for us, but because the Spirit came only subsequent to Jesus' death, then whatever gifts and blessings come to us in the Spirit come to us only *because* of Jesus' death. And since apart from the Spirit there is no life (Jn 6:63), and since without Jesus' death the Spirit does not come, there is no life without *water and blood.* What was at stake in understanding Jesus Christ as the one *who came by water and blood* was an acceptance of his life and death as mediating God's salvation for the world.

The Spirit's Witness to the Son (5:6-9)   Next the Elder turns his attention to the origin of the confession that he came *by water and blood.* It was not concocted by human imagination; rather, *it is the Spirit who testifies.* In evoking the Spirit's testimony the Elder stresses the ultimate source of this confession. He may well do so with an eye to the dissidents, who no doubt claimed their own views to be equally inspired (compare 4:1-6), even if they defied the interpretations that the Elder and his community held "from the beginning" (1:1-4; 2:20-25).

It is helpful to read this part of the epistle with the Gospel in mind. According to the Gospel, one person saw the crucifixion and testified to the water and blood (19:35). This witness is the disciple whom Jesus loved, whom many take to be the founder of the Johannine community and source of the teaching it preserved. He testified both to the fact that water and blood flowed from Jesus' side at his death, as well as to the meaning of that event. When in the epistle we read that it is the *Spirit* who testifies, the Elder is implicitly asserting that the so-called Beloved Disciple's testimony about this event comes from the Spirit (Brown 1982:579; compare Grayston 1984:138).

The insistence that the witness of the Beloved Disciple is identical with the witness of the Spirit arises from the debate in the Johannine community about who truly had the Spirit and what was the content of Spirit-inspired confession. In 1 John 1:1-4, and repeatedly in the rest of the epistle, the author seeks to anchor his teaching in what has been seen, testified to and proclaimed "from the beginning." Precisely that teaching has been and continues to be the result of the anointing of God and the inspiration of the Spirit. Even now the Spirit verifies the testimony of the one who witnessed the event years before. Therefore to reject the witness and teaching of the community that stands in continuity with that disciple's testimony is to spurn the witness of the Spirit. To emphasize the importance of this teaching, the Elder reminds his readers that the Spirit is *the truth*. The Spirit is trustworthy and witnesses to that which is true. Because *the Spirit is the truth,* that disciple's witness also can be trusted.

It is impossible, therefore, that a contrary understanding of the significance of the death of Jesus could be the product of the testimony of the Spirit, for the witness of the Beloved Disciple to the water and blood of Jesus' death is confirmed by the Spirit's ongoing witness to the community. And while John speaks of three witnesses—the Spirit, the water and the blood—in reality he envisions one threefold witness to the fact and significance of Jesus' death. Together, Spirit, water and blood offer one testimony, and the Spirit does not testify without or apart from the blood. The statement that the Spirit, the water and the blood *agree* shows that the Spirit's saving work is not independent of or effective apart from that which was accomplished in Jesus' death.

God's Witness to the Son (5:10-12) Finally, the Elder shifts his

---

5:7 The alternate, longer form of verse 7, given by the NIV as a footnote but found in the KJV, is a later addition to the text, dating no earlier than the third century. For a lengthy discussion, see Brown (1982:775-87).

Some commentators argue that the Spirit, water and blood in verses 7-8 refer to a present or ongoing witness in the community and are not connected with Jesus' historical manifestation. A common interpretation, then, is that *water* and *blood* in these verses refer to the sacraments (even if they did not do so in v. 6; Dodd 1946:131; Haas 1972:120; Houlden 1973:128-30; Schnackenburg 1963:261). But there is no need to posit this change. The three witnesses "remain in the Community as a living testimony to the salvific power of Jesus' death" (Brown 1982:584).

5:9 *[Human] testimony* does not refer to the testimony of the Beloved Disciple. Brown (1982:586) takes it as a reference to John the Baptist's testimony (see Jn 1:32) to the coming of the Spirit at Jesus' baptism, which he conjectures may have been invoked by the seces-

appeal to the highest court: the Spirit's testimony is in fact the testimony of God (5:9, 11), for the Spirit is sent by and from God. Thus rejection of the confession that Jesus *came by water and blood* to give eternal life (v. 11) is not simply doubting a human idea or human word of witness: it is to deny God's own testimony to the Son. And if we are disposed to accept human testimony, as we often are (v. 9), why should we not be willing to accept that testimony which is divine in origin? Indeed, those who reject the testimony of God show that the Spirit is not active within them. For just as the Elder had stated earlier that *we love because [God] first loved us* (4:19), now he argues that our testimony to the world is based on God's prior testimony in our hearts. Therefore, the rejection of this testimony manifests a failure to hear and respond to the witness of God concerning the Son. Those who do not accept this witness to the Son show that they do not have the Spirit of truth, and in their rejection of the Spirit's testimony they as good as deny that the Spirit is speaking the truth; hence, they make God a liar. Nor do they have the eternal life the Son brings, for they have cut themselves off from its source—Jesus, who gave his life for us in death.

The summary of God's testimony with the statement that there is *life in the Son* confirms that what is at stake in the epistle and its various confessions about Jesus is more a soteriological than a specifically christological question. In other words, the issue is not so much "How shall we speak about the person of Jesus Christ?" as it is "Where is salvation, eternal life, to be found, and who has that salvation?" The answer this passage offers is that eternal life comes through appropriating the benefits of Jesus' life-giving death for us. Since the Spirit is the one who bears

---

sionists. But the Gospel of John, although it shows John's subsidiary role to Jesus, would surely view John the Baptist's testimony that the Spirit came upon Jesus, the Son of God, as *God's testimony* (see Jn 1:32-34).

God's testimony is given through the Spirit, water and blood. It is not separate from them (Bruce 1970:121; Dodd 1946:132; Houlden 1973:132; Marshall 1978:240; Smalley 1984:284; Stott 1988:184); but others (Brown 1982:587; Schnackenburg 1963:264) think that the testimony of God is intended as a fourth testimony alongside the other three.

5:11 The NIV, by using a colon to render a Greek *hoti* ("that"), suggests that the content of *God's testimony* is given in the rest of the verse (so also Brown 1982:591; Dodd 1946:133; Stott 1988:185). But other commentators suggest that the end of verse 11 tells us what is the meaning or effect of the testimony (Marshall 1978:241 n. 42; Smalley 1984:287). The two ideas are not antithetical: the one who accepts God's testimony that there is life only through the Son consequently has eternal life (5:12).

witness and inspires understanding of the meaning of Jesus' death, those who acknowledge the community's witness to the meaning of Jesus' death also show that they have the Spirit's testimony within them. Those who stand in continuity with the tradition, not merely for its own sake but because it preserves the centrality of Jesus' death, have salvation *in [the] Son.* The community of the Elder, which has experienced purification and forgiveness through the sacrifice of Jesus (1:7; 2:2; 3:5, 16; 4:10), has God's testimony and so has eternal life.

In summary, then, this passage presents the content of the confession about Jesus Christ that believers are to have and hold. But it also suggests, explicitly and implicitly, how we know the truth. In the final analysis, the truth is known by individuals because God's Spirit guides them into understanding and accepting it (Jn 14:26; 16:13). But appeals to inspiration are always dangerous, because they are so subjective. Aware of this problem, the Elder reminds his readers of a historical event—the blood and water that flowed from Jesus' side at his crucifixion—that was reported and interpreted to them by a trustworthy follower of Jesus, the Beloved Disciple himself. If sometimes the Spirit speaks what seems to be a fresh or new word, then the truth of the testimony ought to be measured against the witness guarded by dependable and faithful individuals and communities, and against the witness of Scripture itself. For the Spirit who guided the original witnesses of events and inspired the interpretation of them does not speak a contrary word to the church today.

□ Closing Exhortations (5:13-21)

Few questions vex faithful believers as much as that of petitionary prayer, especially in view of the extravagant promises in the New Testament that those who ask, receive—whatever they may ask. These promises are always understood to be qualified—one must ask with faith, or one must ask with the qualifier "nevertheless, thy will be done," as Jesus did in

Notes: 5:13 *These things* refer to the content of the entire letter (Brown 1982:608; Culpepper 1985:107; Dodd 1946:133; Haas 1972:124; Houlden 1973:137; Marshall 1978:243) and not only to 5:1-12 (Schnackenburg 1963:273). Nevertheless, 5:6-12 are especially in view as well, for they spell out the author's understanding of the phrase *Son of God* (Smalley 1984:289; Stott 1988:186). As Marshall (1978:243 n. 1) notes, 5:13 sums up the content of the whole epistle, but its function is to link 5:5-11 and 14-21.

his prayer in the Garden of Gethsemane. As C. S. Lewis comments, "[This reservation] makes an enormous difference. But the difference which it precisely does not make is that of removing the prayer's petitionary character" (1963:36). And yet the qualifier "not what I want, but what you want" (Mk 14:36 NRSV) *is* crucial, for it shows us that authentic prayer is the submission of the person to God. As one commentator perceptively notes, "Prayer is not a battle, but a response; its power consists in lifting our wills to God, not in trying to bring his will down to us" (Smalley 1984:295).

The Children of God Have Confidence in Prayer (5:13-17) The passage before us promises believers that *if we ask anything according to [God's] will, he hears us.* It also seems, however, to promise that *whatever we ask* we are granted. The boldness spoken of here is not brashness to challenge the will of God, but the confidence that God's will is done, and that in part it is effected through the prayers of faithful Christians. We turn, then, to this passage both to discern what that will of God is of which John speaks, as well as to inquire what it is that we can pray for with such hope and confidence.

Prayer for Life (5:13-15) In these closing sentences, the Elder is ready to summarize the heart of his concern and his letter, and he does so by assuring his readers that they have eternal life. His primary purpose in writing has been to offer pastoral encouragement, to instill confidence and hope by reminding his readers of the fellowship with God and with each other that they now enjoy. He has comforted them with the thought that, despite the defection of some members of the community, his readers can be assured of inheriting eternal life. Therefore, he urges them to stand fast and to remain loyal in their commitment to God.

The commitment that the Elder entreats them to hold is to *believe in the name of the Son of God.* In trusting themselves to the Son of God, they are granted eternal life as well as the confidence of having that life.

In the Greek, *life* and *eternal* are separated from each other by the verb "have," with a resulting emphasis placed on *eternal.* Similarly, *to you who believe in the name of the Son of God* is placed at the end of the sentence for emphasis.

5:14-15 In these verses, the if-clauses do not project uncertainty or contingency, but are "expectational" (Haas 1972:125) and can be translated "whenever."

To have eternal life is to have fellowship with God (1 Jn 1:2-3; Jn 17:3). "Eternal" means more than "everlasting." As Barclay points out, a life that lasted forever could be an intolerable curse, depending on the quality of that life (1976:113). But eternal life is a blessing and a joy because it is the life of God. Indeed, that is what the adjective "eternal" connotes. Only God enjoys eternal life, but in fellowship with God we share in the life of God. That is what God has given to us in the Son.

Because our fellowship with God is personal and intimate, like the relationship between a loving parent and child, those who have eternal life also have *assurance in approaching God* (or *confidence . . . in approaching God;* compare 2:28; 3:19-23; 4:17). Here the confidence in view is the confidence to come to God in prayer (3:21-23). But we are not merely told that we may *approach* God with confidence, but that we have confidence because we know that God *hears* us. To say that God "hears" prayer means more than that God acknowledges that we have prayed. "Hearing" implies that there is a response, and that the response is favorable. "Hearing" refers to the communication of those who are on intimate and familiar terms with each other (see Jn 5:30; 8:26, 40; 9:31; 11:22; 15:15). Thus in the Gospel of John, Jesus is confident that God always hears him (11:41-42). The promise that God hears us is the assurance that God listens to us favorably and grants us our requests, *whatever we ask.*

There are, however, some qualifications. It is assumed that our prayers will be made *according to [God's] will.* As noted above, this was the qualification of the prayer of Jesus, whose will was always one with that of the Father (Jn 4:34; 5:30), who himself did the will of God in completing the work that brings eternal life (6:38-40) and whose unity with God was manifested in God's "listening" to him (compare 9:30-33; 11:41-42; 12:27-30). That God heard the prayers of Jesus is taken as evidence that Jesus was intimately related to God and that his purpose and mission were at one with the will of God.

There are not many instances in which Jesus is actually shown at

---

5:16 The phrase that the NIV translates *he should pray and God will give him life* reads literally in the Greek, "he will pray, and he will give him life." The pronouns are ambiguous. Clearly the "he" in "he will pray" refers to the one who offers petitions on behalf of the one who sins. But how is "he will give him life" to be construed? There are three options:

prayer in the Gospel of John. Two of them, however, show how Jesus provides the paradigm of prayer for the Christian community. He prays at the tomb of Lazarus for the dead man to return to life, confident that God always hears him (11:41). He prays for his "own," for faithful believers, that they may be protected "from the evil one" (17:15). And in 1 John 2:1, Jesus is referred to as our paraclete, the "one who speaks to the Father in our defense" (see the discussion on 2:1), which refers to his intercessory role on behalf of Christians who sin and confess that sin. Jesus prays for life for his followers—a restoration of life to Lazarus, perseverance for the faithful (Jn 17:15) and forgiveness of sin (1 Jn 2:1), so that they may continue to have life.

By analogy, just as God heard Jesus' prayers because of his obedience and unity with God, so God hears the prayers of the faithful, for they belong to God. But in the context of our passage, one specific kind of request is heard, and that is the petition on behalf of a member of the community who has sinned. The threat to the possession of eternal life is sin (compare v. 16, *sin that leads to death,* and v. 17). Even as Jesus prayed for the perseverance of his followers and continues to intercede for forgiveness, so too is the community charged with the role of interceding for those who confess their sin. God will answer these prayers, and the sinner will be forgiven and kept safe in eternal life (v. 18). Thus the general statements about prayer in verses 14-15 provide the rationale and basis for the particular requests in verses 16-17. The prayer for life for another believer who is committing *a sin that does not lead to death* (v. 16) is not simply one example of the kind of petition God hears; it is precisely the prayer that God hears, even as God answered Jesus' prayers that his followers be given life. For it is the heart of God's will to grant life to those who believe.

Sin unto Death, Sin not unto Death (5:16-17) As a parenthetical aside, John adds the note, *There is a sin that leads to death. I am not saying that he should pray about that.* This statement implies that there are situations in which one is prohibited from praying, a prohibition that

---

(1) The *petitioner* grants the *sinner* life (Bultmann 1973:87 n. 16; Dodd 1946:135; Haas 1972:127; Stott 1988:189). (2) *God* grants the *sinner* life (Brown 1982:611-12; Bruce 1970:124; Marshall 1978:246 n. 171; Schnackenburg 1963:276; Scholer 1975:239-40; Smalley 1984:300; NEB; RSV; NIV). (3) *God* grants life to the *petitioner* (in return for his faithful

seems difficult to comprehend. But it actually fits well with John's understanding of judgment and with the specific kind of prayer to which he
is referring, as we shall see.

First, John draws a distinction in this passage between "sin unto death"
and "sin not unto death." This seems, at first glance, to suggest that some
sins are more serious than others, that in fact they are so severe that they
cannot be forgiven but rather lead one into eternal death. According to
5:16, one may see a fellow Christian *commit a sin that does not lead to
death.* But the passage does *not* explicitly say that it is a fellow believer
committing the sin that *does* lead to death. Indeed, by definition this
seems impossible in the Johannine epistles and particularly in the present context. Sin unto death is sin that carries a person into death's
clutches, into the grip of the evil one (v. 19). And a child of God does
not sin in that way, because one who is truly born of God will rather
manifest that in confession of sin and dependence for forgiveness upon
the atoning work of Christ. But "sin unto death" is already evidence that
one lives in the realm of death, in the world, under the control of the
evil one, and not in the sphere of life and righteousness granted by God
to those who trust in Christ's work on their behalf.

The distinction between kinds of sin is not, therefore, a ranking of the
seriousness of sins that believers commit. Instead, we have here an
implicit distinction between kinds of *sinners* and *sinning.* "Sinning not
unto death" is, paradoxically, sin in the realm of life, committed by one

prayer). While the third option has little support, commentators are fairly well divided on
the first two. The first option, in which the subject of "will give" is the one who prays for
the sinning believer, renders the Greek more naturally. And yet the NIV's insertion of *God*
for "he" accurately reflects Johannine theology, in which it is ultimately God who gives life.

The difference between *sin that leads to death* and *sin that does not lead to death* has
been the subject of much debate; see the catalog of views in Brown 1982:614-19. Interpreters have variously suggested that the *sin that leads to death* is apostasy; blasphemy against
the Holy Spirit; deliberate sin, or "sin with a high hand"; sin that actually leads to physical
death (as in the case of Ananias and Sapphira; Acts 5:1-11; 1 Cor 5:5; 11:29-30; Bruce
1970:124-25); or a specific sin, such as murder, adultery or blasphemy. Others (Brown
1982:617-18; Culpepper 1985:111; Houlden 1973:133-35; Kysar 1986:114-15; Scholer
1975:238; Smith 1991:134-35) suggest that the difference is really to be found in the person
who is sinning since, first of all, a "brother" cannot sin unto death (else he is not a true
"brother") and, second, the distinction between persons fits well with John's dualistic
outlook, which draws sharp lines between the children of God, who have life, and the
children of the devil, who do not have life. When John speaks of those who "sin unto death"
he has in view his own historical context and is referring specifically to the secessionists,

who has eternal life. Some of the epistle's statements (3:4-10; 5:18) could be taken to mean that sinning is evidence that one does not have life. Yet when sins are dealt with in accordance with God's plan to forgive sins—through the prayer for forgiveness and the "atoning sacrifice" of Jesus Christ (1:9; 2:2)—God hears the prayer of one believer for another and so forgives the repentant sinner. The sinner remains in the realm of life. Yet in no way is John sanctioning cheap grace or a licentious lifestyle, for *all wrongdoing is sin.* Indeed, this is why the sins of all— even those who believe in the name of the Son of God and have eternal life—must be confessed and forgiven. But where there is no confession, there is "sinning unto death," sin committed in the realm of death, sin that comes from and leads to death for the one who is guilty of it.

But how does one "see" (5:16) another Christian committing a sin? Does this mean that it is a public or visible sin? Is the Elder referring only to kinds of sins that one can witness, such as actions, rather than thoughts? As is typical of the Johannine literature, "seeing" probably means "perceiving" or "understanding." If one has perceived—and John does not explain how one "perceives" this—that a fellow Christian is sinning, the proper response is to pray for that person. Presumably, that person has also repented and asked for forgiveness, for if the person who is sinning and is to be prayed for is indeed a brother or sister, a fellow Christian, then on John's view they would also be characterized by con- fession of sin and petition for pardon. Those who do not acknowledge

who have left the realm of life. Thus "sin unto death" *appears* to be apostasy; but for John, these people were never truly children of God (2:19-20).

Some interpreters take the phrase *about that (peri ekeinēs)* to go with the verb *saying (legein)* rather than with *should pray (erotan;* Marshall 1978:246; Schnackenburg 1963:278; Scholer 1975:242 n. 61), which yields the following translation: "I am not speaking about that [namely, the sin unto death] now, to say that one should pray for it." This leaves open the possibility of whether one may pray for the one who sins the sin unto death, since the author is merely noting that this is not his concern at present. Marshall (1978:246 n. 19) states emphatically that John is *not* saying, "I say that he should not pray about that," and quotes Brooke (1912:147): "The writer does not forbid such intercession. He merely ab- stains from commanding it." But it is doubtful that the grammar or sense can be construed in this way. Furthermore, the prohibition against intercession is found elsewhere in the Bible (Jer 7:16-18; 11:14; 14:11). In 1 Enoch the ineffectiveness or absence of intercession is viewed as a sign of judgment upon the sinner (1 Enoch 14:4; 97:3, 5). Fourth Ezra speaks of a day when no one may intercede for another (7:102-11). In Jubilees, Noah intercedes for the righteous (10:4), but prays for judgment on the ungodly (10:5-6). First John echoes these traditions that the prohibition against intercession is a sign of judgment upon sinners.

their sins to God are not children of God.

And this gives us a clue why John prohibits prayers for those "whose sin is unto death" (5:16). This prohibition initially seems both hard-hearted and wrong-headed: surely these are precisely the people who most need prayer! The crucial question here is, For *what* is one forbidden to ask? Verse 16 implies that one asks for *life* for the brother or sister who sins, just as Jesus asks for the life of Lazarus (Jn 11:41-43) and for forgiveness for the repentant sinner (1 Jn 2:1). Here, one asks for the confessing sinner to be held steadfast in eternal life (compare 5:18; Jn 17:11-15). Such a prayer can be made because this person (a) continues to be a faithful member of the community ("brother" or "sister"), which implies (b) that this person holds the Johannine confession of Christ and (c) acknowledges the sin to God (1:8—2:2). They have life, and prayer is made that they continue to receive life.

What one may *not* ask for with respect to those whose "sin is unto death" is that they be given life *apart from* their repentance, confession and returning to following Christ. Prohibition of prayer in the Old Testament and Jewish literature roughly contemporaneous with 1 John is a sign of God's judgment on *unrepentant* sinners (compare Jer 7:16-17; 11:14-15). One can pray that unbelievers may repent and come to fellowship with God. But if God were to forgive them as they persist in their sin, that would not be forgiveness: it would be denial of human sinfulness which, in the Elder's view, is an abhorrent lie.

This passage then reflects the other side of John's belief that eternal life is received now: if there is life for believers even now, there is also judgment for unbelievers (Jn 3:16-17). And if the community serves as a vehicle for administering God's life to its members, then it also functions to pronounce judgment. That the Johannine community understood itself to function in just this way is suggested by the words with which the risen Jesus commissioned his disciples: "As the Father has sent me, I am sending you. . . . If you forgive anyone his sins, they are forgiven; if you do not forgive them, they are not forgiven" (Jn 20:21, 23). In any case, the primary will of God is to bring people to life (Jn 3:16), and this is the will of God that Jesus lives out. So too, our wills and purposes are to be one with God in this commission, to be agents of bringing God's forgiveness and eternal life to others. Needless to say, this commission can only be carried out with great humility, with the full recognition that the God who extends forgiveness through the church is a God who is "faithful and just and will forgive us our sins" (1 Jn 1:9), and with caution and pastoral discernment in situations that might be covered by the admonitions here.

Concluding Assurances and Admonitions (5:18-21) Ever pastoral, the Elder closes his letter with three statements of assurance, each beginning *we know* . . . Each statement points to a truth that John affirms as well as to a reality that his readers have experienced. By assuring them that they can properly claim these realities for themselves, the Elder reaffirms to the community its identity as those who are rightly related in fellowship to God. As he does regularly throughout the epistle, he tells his congregation not only what they are to believe, but what belongs to them as children of God. In short, he is eager that they reflect on *who* they are and on *how* they gained their identity.

Several things are said to remind the readers about their identity. They are born of God (v. 18), the children of God (v. 19), those who have understanding, and those who are "in him who is true" (v. 20). These descriptions of who they are predicate an intimate relationship with God, a relationship which depends upon the mediating work of the Son of God (v. 20).

Thus his closing comments aptly summarize what has been said throughout the epistle. It is as if John has heeded the advice often given to writers and speakers that one should "tell them what you're going to tell them, tell them, and then tell them what you've told them." The preface (1:1-4) introduces the theme of the life available to the world, and the epistle develops the implications of how that life is received and what life entails and demands. These concluding verses recapitulate the argument. And yet, even granting the summary nature of 5:18-21, the assertion of the "sinlessness" of those born of God, a sentiment reminiscent of the difficult passage in 3:4-10, follows oddly on the heels of the discussion in vv. 16-17 about the fellow Christian who sins. One might rather have expected a return to the comment that to deny one's sin is to be guilty of making God a liar (1:8-10), while those who confess their sins can be assured of forgiveness. And verse 21 seems to introduce a problem—idol worship—which has not been dealt with previously. Once again the context of this passage is helpful in tracing the author's thought as he summarizes his reflections to his readers.

Confidence in God's Keeping Power (5:18-19) In verses 16-17, the Elder spoke of *a sin that does not lead to death,* which is sin committed by a believer. Again, a believer is by definition not in the realm of death and therefore such sin does not lead to death. The believer does not dwell in the arena that is characterized by sinning, for that realm lies in the grip of the evil one (v. 18). Since believers do not live in the realm of what is evil and false, and so are not held by the power of sin, the Elder can write, *We know that anyone born of God does not continue to sin.* Rather the believer is kept safe, unharmed by the deception and temptations of the evil one.

The statement *the one born of God does not continue to sin* does not mean that the believer has attained some superior moral status or achieved perfection. Rather, because they are born of God, believers are characterized not by sin and death but by truth and life. Being born of God does not grant one a capacity to overcome sin. Rather *born of God* is virtually an equivalent phrase for "does not sin." For *born of God* points to a divine action on our behalf that transfers us to the sphere where the future realities of eternal life are already lived out, even if only

Notes: 5:18 The NIV renders a strong adversative *(alla)* with a semicolon, thus losing the force of the contrast between the first part of the verse *(no one born of God sins)* and the second part (but, *the one who was born of God keeps him safe).* The second statement provides a strong contrast to the first, and virtually restates the first statement in positive terms.

The NIV translates the Greek present tense of *hamartanein* ("to sin") with *continue to sin.* Although *continue* is added in the English translation, it captures the essence of John's view that those born of God do not have sin as their identifying characteristic.

In the statement *the one who was born of God keeps him safe* there is a question whether the *one who was born of God* refers to Jesus (who keeps the believer safe) or to the believer (who keeps himself or herself). Many commentators favor the interpretation that *the one who was born of God* is Jesus (Bruce 1970:126; Bultmann 1973:88; Culpepper 1985:113; Dodd:1946:138; Haas 1972:128; Marshall 1978:252; Scholer 1975:245; Smalley 1984:303; Stott 1988:194), while others opt for a reference to the believer (Brown 1982:622; Houlden 1973:133; Kysar 1986:116; Schnackenburg 1963:280-81). In favor of the second reading is the fact that nowhere else in the Johannine writings is Jesus said to be "born of God." In light of John's theology of the "new birth" or "birth from above" (Jn 3:3, 5), it seems unlikely that the term can refer to the Son of God. Moreover, there might be a parallel between verse 16 (the one who prays for other believers grants them life) and verse 18 (the one who prays

in part. Purity from sin is just such a future expectation now appropriated by believers through trusting in Christ (compare 3:4-10).

Thus in verses 18-19 John's dualistic description of reality comes once again into view. *The one who was born of God keeps him safe* says positively what *and the evil one cannot harm him* formulates in a negative fashion. *We are children of God* contrasts with *and the whole world is under the control of the evil one.* What the children of God have is the assurance that they are held in God's hand, and that "no one can snatch them out of my Father's hand" (Jn 10:28; 17:3, 5). *Touch* means to touch so as to harm (see Job 2:5; Ps 105:15; Zech 2:8). God's children have the assurance that they are guarded and kept by the power of God. They are not immune to temptation nor free from sin. But they are not in the hands of an arbitrary God who on a whim may desert them, nor will they fall under the control of the evil one. Those who are truly children of God cannot lose the life they have in God.

The Coming of the Son of God (5:20-21) Appropriate to the epistle is its concluding statement about the role of the Son of God in bringing salvation and life. The Son of God brings understanding of God and mediates fellowship with him. Jesus has given to us *understanding,* which includes the ability to discern the spirits (4:1-6) and to understand what the Spirit teaches us (2:20-21, 26-27). We are given understanding

---

for another believer thereby keeps that other believer safe).

5:20 To whom does the statement *He is the true God and eternal life* refer? A number of commentators take the *he (houtos)* as referring to God (that is, the Father; so Dodd 1946:140; Grayston 1984:147; Smalley 1984:308; Stott 1988:197-98), but many others think that it refers to Jesus Christ (Barker 1981:357; Brown 1982:626; Bruce 1970:128; Bultmann 1973:90; Haas 1972:129-30; Marshall 1978:254 n. 47; Schnackenburg 1963:291). Although good sense can be made of either reading, a reference to Jesus Christ is supported by the following facts: First, in both the Gospel and epistle, although it is said that God gives eternal life, "life" as a predicate always refers to Jesus Christ (Jn 11:25; 14:6; 1 Jn 1:2); second, the Gospel calls the Word "God" (1:1, 18), as it also does the Risen Christ (20:28). Third, the nearest antecedent of the Greek demonstrative pronoun "this" *(houtos)* is "Jesus Christ."

5:21 Numerous interpretations of *idols* have been suggested (see Brown 1982:627-28). The author probably does not intend a general warning against the worship of pagan idols (Dodd 1946:141), but rather has in view the secessionists' false understandings of God (Barker 1981:357; Brown 1982:628-29; Bruce 1970:128; Culpepper 1985:115; Grayston 1984:148; Houlden 1973:138; Kysar 1986:118; Marshall 1978:257; Smalley 1984:310; Stott 1988:198-99). Schnackenburg (1963:292) understands *idols* against the usage of the term in the Qumran community, where it virtually means "sins" (1 QS 2:11; 17:4-5).

---

of truth, which is not so much the power to understand things as it is the power to know a person, *him who is true.* We see here once again the claim that only through the Son of God can one come to know the God who is true, as opposed to any and every false conception of God that people construct in their own minds. Jesus has come in order that we might come to the knowledge of God who is true. Knowledge of such a God can be mediated only by one who is also characterized by truth (compare Jn 14:6).

In fact the Elder speaks of Jesus not only as *truth* but as *the true God.* John does not mean that all the being or essence of deity is limited to the person of Jesus. But here we do move beyond the assertion that to know the Father is to know the Son; here, to know the Son is to know the Father. This is a bold statement, and virtually a redefinition of the traditional understanding of God (Jn 1:1, 18). Having spelled out in the letter the various false confessions, the Elder caps off the epistle with the highest statement: Jesus Christ is the *true God.* But if Jesus Christ mediates true knowledge of God and is so intimately related to God that he himself can be called *true God,* then any doctrine or worship that dilutes those affirmations is tantamount to idolatry. The warning *little children, keep yourselves from idols* points to the danger of worshiping any God other than the one revealed through Jesus Christ. The idols here are not pagan deities or images of stone or wood. An idol is a false picture of God that causes one to stumble and fall away *from* a relationship with the true God. The Elder's readers are to keep themselves from every kind of false belief, for loyalty to a false god leads to death, but allegiance to the true God brings eternal life.

2 John

How Christian believers are to relate to those who do not believe as they do is a question that has received a number of different answers. Some urge tolerance and charity; others advocate the necessity of guarding the truth and preserving the purity of the church. Second John apparently takes a rather hard line on the matter: *If anyone comes to you and does not bring this teaching, do not take him into your house or welcome him* (v. 10).

To such stern and unrelenting admonitions, C. H. Dodd objects, "Does truth prevail the more if we are not on speaking terms with those whose view of the truth differs from ours—however disastrous their error may be?" (1946:152). How we live together with others in tolerance and charity, while yet preserving the purity of the church and guarding the truth of its proclamation, is one of the knotty problems raised for us by the short epistle we know as 2 John.

The Historical Context 2 John is one of the shortest writings in the New Testament. Its purpose is to deal with the problem of itinerant teachers whose teaching the Elder (v. 1) judges to be false (v. 10) because it denies that *Jesus Christ has come in the flesh* (v. 7; compare 1 Jn 4:2). He warns his readers against sharing in the *wicked work* (v. 11) of these teachers by accepting their beliefs or aiding their propaganda in any way. These false teachers have *gone out into the world* (v. 7; 1 Jn 2:18-19), indicating that they are former church members who have now left the fold and probably are trying to win others to their teaching. Anyone familiar with 1 John will recognize that 2 John encapsulates the situation and problems that lie behind 1 John. But 2 John adds no substantially new content. Why, then, was it written?

It is possible that 2 John served as a cover letter, sent along with 1 John, to include personal greetings from the Elder to a specific congregation in his care. It is also possible that 1 and 2 John were intended for different audiences: 1 John was circulated in the Elder's immediate vicinity, while 2 John was sent to those at a distance, whom the Elder could contact only by letter (v. 12) or by messenger (v. 4). In any case, it is safe to say that the two letters illumine each other and are so obviously written with the same situation in view that each may be used to interpret the other.

Greetings to the Church (vv. 1-3) Unlike 1 John, 2 John has the formal characteristics of a true letter: the sender and recipients are identified and a greeting typical of ancient letters is passed on to them. And yet the identification of the author is unusual, for where one would expect a personal name, the author refers to himself only as *the Elder (ho presbyteros)*. Literally the word means someone who is old, but because those who were old were deemed to have wisdom and experience that qualified them to be leaders, an "elder" was someone who was also in a position of authority (Deut 19:12; Josh 20:4; Ruth 4:2; Ezra 10:4; Acts 11:30; 14:23; 15:2, 23; 16:4; 20:17; Jas 5:14; 1 Pet 5:1; 1 Tim 5:17; Tit 1:5). The *Elder* must have been well known and respected by his readers. He expects them to recognize him without further identification and to follow his instructions. As in 1 John, he speaks of them as *children* (vv. 4, 13), suggesting both the intimacy and the authority he has with them. That he is writing to other congregations suggests that

---

Notes: 1 Some scholars take the term *Elder* to refer to a leader in the church after the generation of the apostles (Brown 1982:651; Dodd 1946:156), which obviously implies that the author of the epistle cannot be the apostle John (see the introduction on "Authorship"). On the Elder's authority and role, see Barker 1981:361; Marshall 1978:60; Smalley 1984:317.

Many commentators hold to the interpretation of *the chosen lady* as a personification of a local church and its members (Barker 1981:361; Brown 1982:654; Bruce 1970:137; Dodd 1946:144; Grayston 1984:152; Houlden 1973:142; Marshall 1978:60; Smalley 1984:318; Smith 1991:139; Stott 1988:204), since the verbs and pronouns of the epistle are all in the plural

his authority extends beyond one local congregation.

The congregation to which he is writing is designated metaphorically as *the chosen lady and her children;* we would say "the church and its members." Regularly in the Scriptures Israel or the church is designated as a woman or the bride of Yahweh or Christ (Is 54:1, 13; Jer 6:21; 31:21; Lam 4:2-3; Jn 3:29; 2 Cor 11:2; Gal 4:25-26; Eph 5:22; Rev 18—19). *Chosen* recalls Jesus' statement in John 15:16, "You did not choose me, but I chose you." The church is not a voluntary organization but the fellowship of those called together by Christ. For such a fellowship, family imagery is all the more appropriate, for it suggests the bonds of intimacy and love that bind the family together. Family imagery also underscores that it was not by the children's initiative that this family came into existence.

In his greeting to the congregation the Elder repeats two important themes: truth (vv. 1-4) and love (vv. 1, 3, 5-6). *Truth* includes matters of both faith and practice, and thus designates what Christians are to believe (v. 7; 1 Jn 4:2; 5:6) and how they are to live (vv. 5-6). Truth is the reality to which Christians are committed, and they are known by their commitment to it.

But that reality is not simply a static and objective entity or set of beliefs. We tend to think of truth as a number of abstract propositions that we are to comprehend and believe. But for the Elder, truth is a vital force that can be personified as living in us and being with us. Because it comes from the living God, truth is a dynamic power that abides with believers, enabling them to know what is true. And because truth comes from God, it exists forever and remains with the faithful, just as God exists eternally and remains in relationship with the faithful. If we could capture John's view of truth as a force that, because it is the work of God's own Spirit, shapes and empowers us, we might be less prone to think

---

("you all"). Moreover, the New Testament elsewhere speaks of the church as a woman or bride, and when greetings are sent from *the children of your elect sister* (v. 13), it suggests the greetings sent from one church to another.

The NIV inserts the definite article in the phrase *whom I love in the truth,* implying the realm of truth in which one loves (Brown 1982:656; Dodd 1946:145; Marshall 1978:62; Stott 1988:202). Others argue for an adverbial interpretation, equivalent to *alēthōs,* "truly" (so NEB; Barker 1981:366 n. 1; Haas 1972:139; Schnackenburg 1963:207). In Johannine thought, one can only love "truly" or "genuinely" if one abides in *the* truth.

of truth as something that depends upon us to preserve it. In reality, we depend upon the truth to guard us—and not vice versa—because we depend upon God. Only as the truth abides in us do we abide in the truth. But we are somewhat too quick to reverse that relationship, and put human beings in the place where God's activity and power belong.

The actual greeting is similar to the somewhat standardized greetings and blessings found in other New Testament epistles (such as Rom 1:7; Gal 6:16; 1 Tim 1:2; 2 Tim 1:2; Jude 2). This is the only use of *mercy* in the Johannine writings. Six other instances of *peace* appear, all in the Gospel of John (14:27; 16:33; 20:19, 21, 26). Peace is the assurance that Christians have in knowing that, whatever the world may bring, they are kept secure in God's love and truth by God's own power (Jn 14:27; 16:33). Surprisingly, *grace* appears elsewhere only in the Gospel of John, and then only in the opening prologue (Jn 1:14, 16-17). Grace summarizes the revelation and salvation that we have received in the Incarnate Word. So while the opening greeting of 2 John may well echo a standard form of greeting, we should understand its content in light of the Christian conception of *grace, mercy and peace,* supremely manifested in God's work in Jesus Christ. Those who live in Christ can be confident that *grace, mercy and peace* will be and are theirs. Thus the greeting is really a promise: *grace, mercy and peace . . . will [always] be with us.*

Living in Love (vv. 4-6)   It was common practice to include a thanksgiving after the greeting of a letter that expressed the writer's pleasure in knowing of the well-being of the addressees. The Elder is "overjoyed" (NRSV) because he has found *some of your children walking* [or *living*]

---

4 Some commentators take the statement that *some of your children [are] living by the truth* as an implicit rebuke to (unnamed) "others" who are not living by the truth (so Barker 1981:363; Dodd 1946:147; Houlden 1973:144; Grayston 1984:153; Smalley 1984:323). Other commentators, however, do not understand it in a negative sense, but see the *some* as consisting of some messengers who have visited the Elder and in whose faith he rejoices (Bruce 1970:139; Marshall 1978:65; Stott 1988:208).

6 In the statement *this is love . . .* most commentators supply as an object "for each other" (for example, Brown 1982:665-66; Marshall 1978:67). But some suggest that the Elder means both love of God and love of others (Barker 1981:363; Smalley 1984:326; Stott 1988:210). In Johannine thought there is no love of God without love of others, and no love of others without love of God; and neither exists apart from obedience to God's command to love. While the expression might seem circular, the thought makes good sense against the back-

in the truth. This does not necessarily imply that other members of the congregation were not living in the truth. But the Elder is acquainted with or has met some who are. And to know that these people are faithful in their commitment to God brings the author joy. The Johannine command to *love one another* inculcates concern for the spiritual welfare of Christian compatriots and joy over their well-being and faithfulness.

The Elder goes on to explicate the *truth* by which they live in terms of the commandment to love each other (compare 1 Jn 3:23). In fact, love is to *live in obedience to [God's] commands*. The love spoken of here includes love for God and love for others. We show that we love God when we do what God desires, and what God desires is that we *live a life of love*. Love is not a feeling or emotion, but a way of life that manifests itself concretely in its concern for others in obedience to the commandments of God. Love circumscribes the whole of life and ought to permeate the actions and attitudes of the Christian person.

Living in Truth (vv. 7-11)   If Christian existence can be characterized as "living in love," it can equally be designated as a life that is lived in truth, where truth is the opposite of deception and wickedness. Truth is both doctrinal and moral in scope. The previous section (vv. 4-6) dealt with the moral aspect of truth; the present section turns to the question of doctrinal truth and, specifically, true confession of Jesus Christ.

The confession *Jesus Christ has come in the flesh* is identical in emphasis, although not in wording, to the confession of 1 John 4:2. This confession calls attention to Jesus' true and full humanity and to the significance of his life *in the flesh*. For it was as the one who became

---

ground of John's understanding of love.

The plural *commands* should not be construed to mean "the detailed requirements" that explicate the central command to love (Marshall 1978:67; Smalley 1984:326). The Elder here alternates between the plural and singular as does 1 John, and even 1 John 3:23 uses the singular "command" to refer to the twin commands to love and to believe. In this instance, *command* refers to *love one another,* and *commands* may refer either to the dual focus of 1 John 3:23, or to the other central tenets of Johannine faith (to hold to the truth, walk in love and keep the commands).

7 Although many commentators interpret *world* with a neutral sense as the public sphere in which Christians live (Bultmann 1973:112; Dodd 1946:148; Marshall 1978:69 n. 4; Smalley 1984:328; Stott 1988:211), Brown (1982:668) is correct that this is not strong enough. *World* has here a negative connotation, as that which stands opposed to the church, the ungodly

flesh (Jn 1:14) that he revealed the glory of God, and it was his flesh that he gave for the life of the world (Jn 6:51). It was also as a human being that he modeled the life of obedience to God and love for others that is commanded throughout the epistles (2 Jn 6; 1 Jn 3:23). In short, this confession summarizes who Jesus is and what he has done for our salvation: he became flesh, and he gave that flesh in death so that we might have life. Those who are called *deceivers* and *antichrists* have left the sphere of truth for the sphere known as the world—that arena which rejects the work of Christ on its behalf. By leaving the church and going out into the world, they have shown that they rejected the salvation that Jesus brings and have disobeyed the commandment to maintain the bonds of love with other Christians.

The Elder urges his readers not to commit the same error as those who have *gone out into the world,* but to see that *you do not lose what you have worked for.* This admonition can be illuminated by setting it against the Gospel of John. The verb that is translated *lose* is found in several instances in the Gospel, where it refers to being lost (6:39; 17:12; 18:9) and to perishing (3:16; 10:28). Those whom Jesus has chosen cannot be lost; those who do not accept Jesus as God's provision for salvation are perishing. These are the only options. There is no way to have a little bit of life or death; one either lives or dies. To *lose what you have worked for* is to lose life. It would be to abandon one's commitment to God. For the *work* in view is the act of faith. As Jesus says in the Gospel of John, the "work of God" is "believing in the one [whom God] has sent" (6:29). The deceivers who have gone out into the world have not continued in believing "in the one [whom God] has sent."

---

sphere into which one enters when one leaves the fellowship of Christ (1 Jn 2:15-17; Culpepper 1985:122; Smalley 1984:328).

The NIV translates the confession of verse 7 as *Jesus Christ has come in the flesh,* thus rendering it identical to a similar confession in 1 John 4:2, where the tense of the verb differs; here it is present, there it is perfect. Many commentators suggest that the present tense lays emphasis on the lasting, permanent union of the two natures of Christ (Barker 1981:364; Marshall 1978:70-71 and n. 7; Stott 1988:212). The RSV, supported by Bruce (1970:141), translates "the coming of Jesus Christ in the flesh," suggesting that the Incarnation is in view (see Smalley 1984:329, "Jesus Christ, incarnate"). Brown (1982:670) accounts for the present tense here by suggesting that the Elder may be quoting a stereotyped expression, since the Messiah is spoken of as "the coming one" in John (Jn 1:15, 27; 12:13). The formulations of 1 John 4:2 and 2 John 7 both use confessional or creedal language and, despite the difference in the form of the verb, surely have the same thrust. That the same

So the Elder cautions his readers not to follow their example or to be swayed by their superficially progressive teaching. Even more, the Johannine Christians are not to welcome into their house anyone who comes with this deceptive teaching. The refusal to welcome the false teachers into one's home is a sign of judgment upon their teaching and life. And if the *house* in question is not merely a personal residence but rather a house *church*, then the Elder forbids them to be given entrance into the church so as to teach the people.

Anyone who welcomes him shares in his wicked work means more than "you are known by the company you keep." Rather, to give false teachers a hearing is to further their work and so to be equally guilty of false teaching. The word translated by the NIV as *shares* is more literally translated "to share fellowship with," and it is an important idea in the Johannine community. First John spoke of having fellowship with God and his Son, just as Christians have fellowship with each other (1:3). These are not passing acquaintances, but deep and life-shaping relationships. The Johannine Christians are not to share such fellowship with those who do not speak the truth.

This brings us back to the question that C. H. Dodd raised: "Does truth prevail the more if we are not on speaking terms with those whose view of the truth differs from ours—however disastrous their error may be?" Dodd's query raises an important point, but is it the right question? It is difficult, if not impossible, to know exactly what the personal and social relationships were between the Christians of the Elder's congregation and those who had withdrawn from it. Were the Christians of John's community actually "not on speaking terms" with those who had

---

confession can be couched either in the present or in the perfect tense suggests that the meaning of the confession does not rest on the tense of the verb. The issue is not the permanent relation of the "two natures" of Christ nor of the nature of the Incarnation itself, but is rather the importance of confessing "Jesus Christ Incarnate." "Incarnate" can translate the confession of 1 John 4:2 (perfect tense) and 2 John 7 (present tense).

9 *Teaching of Christ* may mean "doctrine *about* Christ" (Bultmann 1973:113; Marshall 1978:72 n. 13; Smalley 1984:332; Smith 1991:145) or "instruction *from* Christ" (Brown 1982:674-75; Bruce 1970:142; Schnackenburg 1963:314; Stott 1988:214). One can make good sense of either option. The reference to the command to love (v. 6) suggests "instruction from Christ," while the reference to confessing that *Jesus Christ has come in the flesh* supports the translation "doctrine about Christ," which reflects the situation of conflict in the Johannine churches.

left the church? Had they tried to win back those under the sway of the false teachers? Were their attitudes and actions cold and judgmental? We have no way of answering these kinds of questions.

We do know, however, that the Elder categorically refused to compromise his beliefs or to allow the false teachers to gain a hearing at all. Some might label such actions intolerant and haughty. After all, how can the Elder be sure that he indeed knows the truth? In fact, his confidence rests in his belief that God has revealed what is true in the Son, Jesus Christ (v. 3), and that the Holy Spirit enables him to know and hold to his confession of faith. Truth is neither an arbitrary construct of the human mind nor impossibly obscure. Christians need not fear that they have somehow missed the truth or failed to understand it, that there is some key that unlocks the mysteries of knowing God that they have been missing all along. Such a "key" may have been promised by the false teachers, but to John they are not revealing the heart of the truth but are rather *run[ning] ahead* of (or "going beyond," RSV) the truth.

And what of the charge of intolerance? As Kysar notes, "Tolerance must finally have its limits, if the church is to have integrity" (1986:133). We would do well to take note of the corporate focus of the Elder's concern, for he is particularly worried lest the false teachers be granted an opening to teach and propagate their doctrine within the church. It is the church's responsibility to teach people and to nurture them in faith, righteousness and love. As a church, it must draw the lines that exclude teaching and practice it deems out of harmony with the revelation of the Scripture. It has this right and responsibility. To be sure, in the effort to guard truth with zeal, some churches draw the lines too soon and too narrowly. But in the effort to exhibit Christian charity and tolerance, some churches refuse to draw the line at all. The continuing challenge to the church is to "speak the truth in love." Unfortunately, as one wag has said, this generally leads to a lot of speaking, little truth and even less love!

Closing Greetings (vv. 12-13) Ancient secular letters often include an expression of desire to see the recipients of the letter, as is found in the closing greetings of 2 John. A face-to-face visit will complete *our joy.* If the author is not simply speaking in the editorial "we," then the plural refers to him and the community with him. Indeed, this is what the closing verse suggests, for the *children of your chosen sister* are the Christians of the local church from which the Elder is writing. Their joy, the Elder's joy and the joy of the recipients—*our joy*—will be completed. "Completed joy" is joy that has reached its goal in fellowship with each other and with God. Again the mutual interdependence of Christians, so important to the Johannine community, comes to expression in the simplest way, in a farewell greeting to a church. For the greeting is not simply from an isolated writer, even one so well known as *the Elder*, but from one church to another. "Beloved, let us love one another" was not simply an external obligation, but the inner directive by which these believers lived.

3 John

The epistle known as 3 John is the shortest letter in the New Testament. Like 2 John, it is from *the Elder* but, unlike 2 John, it is addressed to an individual—Gaius—and not to a local congregation, although the letter may well have been intended for a wider audience. The purpose of 3 John is to encourage Gaius to continue extending hospitality to traveling emissaries, especially those who come from the Elder or who are loyal to him. In particular, the Elder urges Gaius' reception of one missionary named Demetrius (v. 12). It may well be that Demetrius is carrying 3 John to Gaius and that the letter serves as something of an introduction of and reference for Demetrius. The Elder must call Gaius to his aid since an individual named Diotrephes—who is apparently exerting considerable influence—has placed himself in opposition to the Elder by failing to support the Elder's messengers. The Elder has already written one letter to the congregation of which Diotrephes is a part (v. 9), but apparently that letter was ignored. So the Elder now turns to Gaius, and asks for him to undertake the work of hospitality that Diotrephes has refused to do (vv. 9-10).

Notes: 1 For comments on *the Elder,* see the notes on 2 John 1.

There is no evidence to support Marshall's contention (1978:83) that Gaius was not in the best of health, and the standardized form of this prayer in ancient letters argues against it.

2 The NIV renders *psychē* with *soul* here, but in the Gospel of John it translates the same word as "life" (10:11, 15, 17; 12:25), in the sense of a life that one can give up or lay down,

Living in Truth (vv. 1-2) Typical of ancient letters (and like 2 John) 3 John begins with an identification of its author and intended recipient, followed by a thanksgiving and then a wish for the well-being of the recipient. Third John lacks a greeting such as that found in 2 John 3 (but compare v. 14) and other New Testament epistles, but such a lack does not suggest that the Elder is angry with or lacks affection for Gaius. The Elder addresses Gaius as *my dear friend.* While *dear friend* suggests cordiality, it is probably not strong enough to capture the meaning of the Greek word "beloved" *(agapētos)*, found as an address to the readers throughout 1 John (2:7; 3:21; 4:1, 7). For love is not simply affection or attachment, but the God-given bond that unites Christians. And the Elder's statement that he loves Gaius *in the truth* points to the double-stranded cord that unites them: they are held together not only by love but also by the truth that they share in common.

The wish for health is also typical of ancient letters and here is really a prayer. Specifically, the Elder's prayer is that *all may go well with you, even as your soul is getting along well.* The word translated "soul" *(psychē)* refers to the whole being of a person. In the Gospel of John, Jesus is said to lay down his *psychē,* which certainly means more than to give his "soul" (compare Jn 10:15, 17-18). The author's confidence that Gaius is *getting along well* with respect to his soul would not simply point to a state of having one's soul saved, but rather to spiritual and moral health as evidenced in holding to the correct confession of Jesus and living in obedience to the commands of God and, particularly, to the command to love. In other words, "spiritual health" is to *continue to walk in the truth* (v. 3).

Working Together with the Truth (vv. 3-8) Another standard feature of ancient letters is the thanksgiving (2 Jn 4; Rom 1:8-9; 1 Cor 1:4-5; 2 Cor 1:3-4; and so forth). While such expressions of thanksgiving are common, naturally their content will vary with the individuals and sit-

---

as opposed to eternal life *(zōē),* which cannot be lost. In John 10:25 and 12:27 it refers to the part of the human being capable of emotion.

Translations that read "that you may prosper . . ." have allowed for the unfortunate and misguided interpretation that what the author intends is material prosperity for all Christians; for the theological objections to this viewpoint see Stott 1988:223. For parallels to this wish in non-Christian correspondence, see Dodd 1946:158.

uation. Here we learn something about the occasion of 3 John. Christians who have come from Gaius' region or congregation have reported to the Elder and his church of the faithfulness of Gaius. These Christians may be itinerant preachers of the Johannine community who themselves experienced the hospitality for which Gaius was known. They may even have experienced Diotrephes' refusal of hospitality (v. 9). At any rate, word has come to the Elder of Gaius' *faithfulness to the truth*.

On the surface, it may seem to be an exaggeration to speak of hospitality as a mark of *faithfulness to the truth* and living *according to the truth*. *Hospitality* means more than providing an occasional dinner or offering a room for a night, although it may certainly include these things. The *hospitality* of which the Elder speaks means financial assistance and support to missionaries of the Christian gospel so that they may fulfill the vocation to which God called them. Gaius was offering help to preachers of the gospel, thereby supporting the propagation of the truth as well as implying his affirmation of their work. Such support is the obligation of Christians, who together are named by *the Name* of Jesus. Just as missionaries have gone out *for the sake of the Name,* so those who support the missionaries do so *for the sake of the Name.* Together they further the cause of Jesus. They *work together for the truth:* some by preaching, some by supporting the preacher. Support of the Christian mission is not the responsibility or concern of *pagans* or unbelievers. But for the Christian it is both a Christian duty and an act of Christian love.

By his support of these itinerant preachers, Gaius was living in obedience to the truth, which mandated love for one another based on the command and example of Jesus Christ. Gaius' generosity put into prac-

---

6 There are two references to *the church* (here, and v. 9). Each refers to a local congregation. Here the reference is to a church in the Elder's vicinity, where Christians have come or returned following their travels. In verse 9 the *church* is clearly the church of which Diotrephes is part. What is not clear is whether Gaius is a member of the same congregation. Although some commentators assume that he is (Marshall 1978:88; Stott 1988:229), why does the Elder have to tell Gaius what Diotrephes is doing if they belong to the same fellowship? Various suggestions have been made: Gaius is the head of another house church in the same area (Malherbe 1977:222-32); he lives at some distance from the church, and so is not intimately acquainted with the details of what is going on there (Marshall 1978:88); the Elder simply repeats what Diotrephes is doing to underscore the evil behavior that Gaius is not to imitate (Brown 1982:729); or, perhaps, Gaius is a member—not a leader—of

tice the admonition of 1 John 3:16-17 that Christians give of their material possessions for each other. Even though he had not previously known these fellow Christians, that they were fellow believers, themselves faithful to the truth, was adequate reason for extending hospitality and support. Once again the strength of the bond of love between fellow believers comes to expression.

The Elder's response to this situation is to rejoice. For the faithfulness to the truth that Gaius demonstrates and that the Elder praises is not merely intellectual assent to a body of beliefs, nor a disembodied commitment to an abstract truth. It is rather wholehearted allegiance to God's truth as manifested in concrete actions to specific individuals. Such commitment elicits the greatest of joy (compare 2 Jn 4). Anyone who has been teacher, guide, mentor or parent to another can resonate with the Elder's expression of joy that his children, those in his care and for whom he is responsible, are *living according to the truth*. The somewhat stern and anxious tone of the Elder is softened by this expression of joy and gratitude for all that Gaius is *doing for [fellow Christians]*.

Imitating Truth (vv. 9-12) Because Gaius is *walking in the truth* (v. 4), he is worthy of imitation. By contrast, Diotrephes serves as an example that ought not to be imitated. The epistle provides only the barest of hints about who Diotrephes was and what he was doing. Several charges are raised against him: he *loves to be first;* he will *have nothing to do* with the Elder and *gossips maliciously* about him; and he *refuses to welcome the brothers.* Diotrephes has failed to provide hospitality and, even more, financial assistance and other kinds of support for itinerating Christian preachers in his area. The charge that *he will have nothing to*

---

another church near Diotrephes' church (Brown 1982:731).

7 The *pagans* are not Gentiles, but unbelievers. The same contrast between "brothers" and "pagans" is found in Matthew 5:47; 18:15-17.

8 The phrase "working for the truth" can also be translated "working with the truth" (so Brown 1982:714; Bruce 1970:151; Dodd 1946:160; Marshall 1978:87; Smalley 1984:352; Stott 1988:228). Dodd suggests "prove ourselves allies of the truth." The emphasis is not so much on working in order to further the cause of truth, but working in harmony with the truth, already at work by God's power in the world.

9 Few commentators today argue that what the author is referring to in the statement *I wrote to the church* is either 1 or 2 John (but see Grayston 1984:160, who suggests that it is 2 John). Most take it as another letter, now lost.

do with the Elder suggests that the Christians whom he will not support are emissaries from the Elder, who have come to help the church in various ways.

But why does Diotrephes refuse to welcome these Christians? Because the Elder raises no charges against Diotrephes' orthodoxy or beliefs, the issue between them is not doctrinal. Diotrephes is not one of the false teachers or prophets referred to in 1 and 2 John (1 Jn 2:18; 4:1). The Elder does not brand him as *antichrist.* Neither is Diotrephes one of the secessionists. He has not left the community to start his own fellowship. He has remained within the greater Johannine community. And yet he has refused to welcome other Christians from that community, and precisely because they come from the Elder.

Evidently the Elder and Diotrephes are engaged in a struggle for authority in the congregation to which Diotrephes belongs. That the Elder believes he has the right to challenge Diotrephes' power suggests that this congregation was founded by the Elder's efforts, either directly or indirectly. But it is not clear what Diotrephes' official role is in the local congregation. He may, for example, be the designated or official leader of one house church. Or perhaps he is an influential lay-leader within that house church or among several house churches. He has sufficient power to prevent the church as a whole from welcoming the traveling missionaries. The charge that he *loves to be first* suggests that he has power and, from the Elder's point of view, delights in throwing his weight around. But it is not clear from the letter whether he has gained this power legitimately or has usurped it. Whatever his role, Diotrephes rejects the Elder's assertion of responsibility for the congregation, ignoring his letters and rejecting his messengers.

While most commentators do not think that Diotrephes is guilty of heresy (Brown 1982:706; Bruce 1970:152; Bultmann 1973:101; Dodd 1946:165; Smith 1991:154; Stott 1988:229), some do (Houlden 1973:153; Smalley 1984:364-65). But the Elder would surely have called attention to Diotrephes' doctrinal errors had he been guilty of them.

The charge that Diotrephes *loves to be first* does not mean that Diotrephes merely *wants* to be first, but that he is actually exercising authority in the local congregation (Brown 1982:717). Houlden's translation as "power-hungry" (1973:153) captures the emotional force of the statement. But more than an inner attitude is in view.

10 There has been much speculation about the church structures of the Johannine community, the role of the Elder and the authority of Diotrephes. Dodd writes that the Elder's statement that he *will call attention to what [Diotrephes] is doing* suggests that the Elder

The author's words about Diotrephes may seem harsh, especially when it is not clear that Diotrephes has done anything other than oppose the Elder and his messengers. And yet we must note that the Elder does not speak of Diotrephes as antichrist, as a false prophet or as failing to abide in the congregation or to hold to the truth, all of which were accusations leveled against the secessionists of 1 and 2 John. It is possible that 3 John is an example of the Elder's response and warning to one whom he does not regard as in the darkness, and yet whose actions need to be conformed more closely to the sphere of light. Certainly the Elder does not approve of Diotrephes' actions. For Diotrephes' failure to support the Elder is not just a personal affront; it is an assault against the unity of Christian fellowship. That the Elder attacks such schismatic tendencies with the same vigor that he warns against doctrinal error surely has a message of warning for independent-minded Christians today.

Gaius is urged to steer clear of Diotrephes' influence and shun his example. Instead, Gaius is to imitate *what is good. Good* here is not a general category of "good things," but specifically the good that comes from God, that is in harmony with God's character and in keeping with God's actions. Above all, that *good* is the good of love modeled and inspired by God. "Let us love one another, for love is of God" (1 Jn 4:7; 3:10; 4:20). Love for others demonstrates both love for God and the indwelling love of God flowing through that person. The call to imitate what is good, what is *from God,* will be heeded only by those who are also *from God.* For those who have not come into fellowship with God cannot live out the good.

The statement *anyone who does what is evil has not seen God* calls to

---

is not sure of his ground (1946:165). He cannot simply rally the congregation to his side by his command, nor does he have the power or authority to forbid Diotrephes' activities. On the other hand, Grayston points out that the preservation of 3 John suggests that in the end the Elder triumphed and that his efforts were successful (1984:162).

12 The statement that Demetrius is *well spoken of by everyone,* even by *the truth itself* has been variously interpreted. Bruce (1970:155) suggests that *the truth itself* can be paraphrased as "the facts themselves," while others view *the truth* as the manifestation of truth in Demetrius' own style of life (Smalley 1984:361; Stott 1988:233), or as a personification of truth (Marshall 1978:93, "if truth could speak"). The point is that Demetrius is living *according to the truth,* and so the truth in turn serves as a witness on his behalf.

---

3 JOHN 13-14 □

mind 1 John 4:20, where the Elder stated that love for an unseen God demands love for the very visible fellow believer. Here, then, John means that failure to do right, to love one's fellow Christian, manifests a lack of understanding of and fellowship with the God who is love. And if Diotrephes is an example to avoid, Demetrius is *well spoken of by everyone,* a translation that is perhaps too weak. The Greek conveys the sense that Demetrius has faithful and true witnesses who will attest to his character. Even *the truth itself* joins in this testimony. The truth that he professed and adhered to was embodied in him in such a way that he needed no further witnesses. And yet both other Christians and the Elder himself are willing to speak on his behalf.

Closing Greetings (vv. 13-14) The Elder's closing greetings echo those of 2 John 12. These greetings show, once again, the high premium placed on Christian love and fellowship. While 3 John does not include the formulaic greeting, "grace, mercy and peace from God the Father and from Jesus Christ" (2 Jn 3), the simple *peace to you,* when coupled with the greeting that Gaius is one whom the Elder *loves in the truth* (v. 1), expresses the same heartfelt prayer. Gaius will have peace as he abides in the truth (v. 1) and shares in the fellowship of love that comes from God and binds believers to one another.

Bibliography

Barclay, W.
1976   *The Letters of John and Jude.* Rev. ed. Philadelphia:
            Westminster.
Balz, H.
1980   *Die Johannesbriefe.* Neues Testament Deutsch. Göttingen:
            Vandenhoeck und Ruprecht.
Barker, G. W.
1981   "1 John, 2 John, 3 John." *The Expositor's Bible Commentary.*
            Edited by F. Gaebelein. Grand Rapids, Mich.: Zondervan.
            12:293-377.
Bonhoeffer, D.
1959   *The Cost of Discipleship.* New York: Macmillan.

Brooke, A. E.
1912   *A Critical and Exegetical Commentary on the Johannine*
            Epistles. International Critical Commentary. Edinburgh: T. &
            T. Clark.
Brown, R. E.
1982   *The Epistles of John.* Anchor Bible. Garden City, N.Y.:
            Doubleday.

Bruce, F. F.
1970   *The Epistles of John.* Grand Rapids, Mich.: Eerdmans.

Buechner, F.
1973   *Wishful Thinking. A Theological ABC.* New York: Harper &
                Row.

Bultmann, R.
1973   *The Johannine Epistles.* Hermeneia. Philadelphia: Fortress.
1974   *"γινώσκω." Theological Dictionary of the New Testament.*
                10 vols. Edited by G. Kittel and G. Friedrich. Grand Rapids:
                Eerdmans. 1:689-719.

Busch, E.
1976   *Karl Barth. His Life from Letters and Autobiographical Texts.*
                Philadelphia: Fortress.

Calvin, J.
1961   *St. John: Part Two. The Gospel According to St. John 11—21
                and the First Epistle of John.* Calvin's New Testament
                Commentaries. Edited by D. W. Torrance and T. F. Torrance.
                Grand Rapids, Mich.: Eerdmans.

Cullmann, O.
1963   *The Christology of the New Testament.* Rev. ed. Philadelphia:
                Westminster.

Culpepper, R. A.
1985   *1 John, 2 John, 3 John.* Knox Preaching Guides. Atlanta:
                John Knox.

Delling, G.
1972   *"τέλος." Theological Dictionary of the New Testament.* 10
                vols. Edited by G. Kittel and G. Friedrich. Grand Rapids,
                Mich.: Eerdmans. 8:49-87.

Dodd, C. H.
1946   *The Johannine Epistles.* The Moffatt New Testament
                Commentary. New York: Harper & Brothers.

Dunn, J. D. G.
1980   *Christology in the Making. A New Testament Inquiry into the
                Origins of the Doctrine of the Incarnation.* Philadelphia:
                Westminster.

Grayston, K.
1984   *The Johannine Epistles.* New Century Bible. London:
                Marshall, Morgan & Scott; Grand Rapids, Mich.: Eerdmans.

Haas, C.,
M. DeJonge and
J. L. Swellengrebel

1972   *A Translator's Handbook on the Letters of John.* London:
        United Bible Societies.

Houlden, J. L.

1973   *The Johannine Epistles.* Harper's New Testament
        Commentary. New York: Harper & Row.

Kysar, R.

1986   *I, II, III John.* Augsburg Commentary on the New Testament.
        Minneapolis: Augsburg.

La Rondelle, H. K.

1971   *Perfection and Perfectionism. A Dogmatic-Ethical Study of
        Biblical Perfection and Phenomenal Perfectionism.* Berrien
        Springs, Mich.: Andrews University Press.

Lewis, C. S.

1952   *Mere Christianity.* New York: Macmillan.
1963   *Letters to Malcolm: Chiefly on Prayer.* New York: Harcourt,
        Brace & World.

Longenecker, R.

1970   *The Christology of Early Jewish Christianity.* Grand Rapids,
        Mich.: Baker.

Luther, M.

1971   *Luther's Works: Word and Sacrament IV.* Vol. 38. Edited by
        M. E. Lehman. Philadelphia: Fortress.

Malherbe, A. J.

1977   "The Inhospitality of Diotrephes." *God's Christ and His
        People. Festschrift for Nils Ahlstrup Dahl.* Edited by J. Jervell
        and W. Meeks. Oslo: Universitet, pp. 222-32.

Marshall, I. H.

1978   *The Epistles of John.* New International Commentary on the
        New Testament. Grand Rapids, Mich.: Eerdmans.

Morris, L.

1970   "1 John, 2 John, 3 John." *The New Bible Commentary:
        Revised.* Leicester, England: Inter-Varsity Press; Grand
        Rapids, Mich.: Eerdmans, pp. 1259-73.

Moule, C. F. D.

1959   *An Idiom Book of New Testament Greek.* Cambridge:
        Cambridge University Press.

Plummer, A.
1896   *The Epistles of S. John. With Notes, Introduction and Appendices.* The Cambridge Bible for Schools and Colleges. Cambridge: Cambridge University Press.

Schnackenburg, R.
1963   *Die Johannesbriefe.* Herders theologischer Kommentar zum Neuen Testament. Freiburg: Herder.

Scholer, D. M.
1975   "Sins Within and Sins Without: An Interpretation of 1 John 5:16-17." *Current Issues in Biblical and Patristic Interpretation.* Edited by G. F. Hawthorne. Grand Rapids, Mich.: Eerdmans, pp. 230-46.

Smalley, S. S.
1984   *1, 2, 3 John.* Word Biblical Commentary. Waco, Tex.: Word Books.

Smith, D. Moody
1991   *First, Second and Third John.* Interpretation: A Bible Commentary for Teaching and Preaching. Louisville, Ky.: John Knox Press.

Stott, J. R. W.
1988   *The Letters of John.* Tyndale New Testament Commentaries. Leicester, England: Inter-Varsity Press; Grand Rapids, Mich.: Eerdmans.

Trites, A. A.
1978   "Witness." *Dictionary of New Testament Theology.* 4 vols. Edited by C. Brown. Grand Rapids, Mich.: Zondervan. 3:1047-50.

Westcott, B. F.
1883   *The Epistles of John. The Greek Text with Notes.* London: Macmillan.